Language to go

STUDENTS' BOOK

Antonia Clare

JJ Wilson

Series Editor: Simon Greenall

Longman

www.longman.com

www.language-to-go.com

Present/future

Lesson 1 Getting ahead p.4
Language to go: Talking about your job/hobby
Speaking and vocabulary: Your life
Listening: Chris's career
Grammar: Review of tenses
Get talking and writing: Achievements and hobbies

Vocabulary 1

Lesson 2 Modern survival p.6
Language to go: Discussing health and lifestyles
Speaking and vocabulary: Adjectives for describing lifestyles
Listening: Radio interview with doctor
Vocabulary 2: Verb phrases to describe health
Get talking and writing: Lifestyles

The past

Lesson 3 Coincidences p.8
Language to go: Telling stories in the past
Vocabulary and speaking: Time adverbials
Reading and speaking: *You'll never believe it!*
Grammar: Narrative tenses
Get talking and writing: Important events

Connecting

Lesson 4 Friends p.10
Language to go: Discussing advantages and disadvantages
Vocabulary and speaking: Noun combinations with -friend and -mate
Listening: Radio interview with a counsellor
Grammar: Phrases of addition, result and contrast
Get talking and writing: Friendship

Verb patterns

Lesson 5 Small talk p.12
Language to go: Making small talk at a party
Vocabulary and speaking: Ways of talking
Reading: *Conversation stunners*
Listening: Types of conversation
Grammar: Question tags
Get talking: Roleplay: at a party

Vocabulary 2

Lesson 6 True love p.14
Language to go: Talking about a relationship
Vocabulary and speaking: Expressions for describing relationships
Reading and speaking: Nelson/Winnie Mandela and Liz Taylor/Richard Burton
Vocabulary 2: Phrasal verbs 1
Get talking and writing: Story-telling

Modals

Lesson 7 The daddy of discipline p.16
Language to go: Discussing ways of bringing up children
Vocabulary and speaking: Phrases to describe behaviour
Reading: *Seven ways to be a good parent*
Grammar: Obligation verbs
Get talking: Seven commandments

Functions

Lesson 8 That's funny p.18
Language to go: Discussing what makes you laugh
Speaking and vocabulary: Humour
Listening: Four people say what makes them laugh
Functions: Agreeing, disagreeing, giving and asking for opinions
Get talking: What humour do you like?

Lesson 9 A perfect weekend p.20
Language to go: Making plans
Vocabulary and speaking: Weekend activities
Reading: E-mails
Grammar: Tenses for describing future plans
Get talking and writing: A day trip

Lesson 10 Just the job p.22
Language to go: Writing a CV
Speaking and reading: *Getting your foot in the door*
Vocabulary: Expressions for describing yourself, your skills and experience
Get writing: Job applications and CVs

Lesson 11 In the media p.24
Language to go: Having a job interview and talking about your experience
Vocabulary and speaking: The media
Listening: A job interview
Grammar: Present perfect simple/continuous
Get talking: Job interviews

Lesson 12 Ready to cook! p.26
Language to go: Describing how to make a dish
Speaking and vocabulary: Preparing and cooking food
Listening and speaking: Two recipes
Grammar: Countable/uncountable nouns and quantifiers
Get talking: Recipes

Lesson 13 Contact p.28
Language to go: Discussing social behaviour
Speaking and vocabulary: Expressions to describe gestures
Reading: *Why Britain suffers a kissing crisis*
Grammar: The -ing form/infinitive
Get talking: Social acceptability

Lesson 14 Two cities p.30
Language to go: Describing places
Speaking and listening: Promotional video on Birmingham
Vocabulary: Geographical location and character
Get talking and writing: Location and brochure for an international conference

Lesson 15 Round the clock p.32
Language to go: Talking about consequences
Vocabulary and speaking: Verb + noun combinations to describe work patterns and habits
Reading: *24 hours a day*
Grammar: Zero, first and second conditionals
Get talking: Attitudes to getting up early and staying up late

Lesson 16 Person to person p.34
Language to go: Talking about people you know
Vocabulary and speaking: Adjectives for describing people's characters
Listening: *Let's Date!* TV programme
Function: Describing personality
Get talking and writing: Blind dates for six famous people

Lesson 17 Positive thinking p.36
Language to go: Talking about how likely things are to happen
Vocabulary and speaking: Weather idioms used for personality
Reading and speaking: *Optimist or pessimist?*
Grammar: Expressions of probability
Get talking: Predictions, optimism and pessimism

Lesson 18 Money talks p.38
Language to go: Talking about money
Vocabulary and speaking: Expressions with *money*
Listening: Bruce and Vlad discuss different aspects of money
Vocabulary 2: Financial terms
Get talking: Attitudes to money

Lesson 19 Unlucky for some p.40
Language to go: Talking about things you were going to do
Vocabulary and speaking: Disaster verbs and prepositions
Reading: Four tales of misfortune
Grammar: Future in the past
Get talking and writing: Tales of woe

Lesson 20 Taxi! p.42
Language to go: Talking about journeys
Speaking and listening: Taxis in different countries
Vocabulary: Adverbs of intensity
Grammar: *So/such*
Get talking: Memorable journeys

Lesson 21 Major events p.44
Language to go: Describing important events
Vocabulary: News, events and disasters
Speaking and listening: Important 20th-century events
Grammar: Passives
Get talking: Major events

Lesson 22 Street life p.46
Language to go: Talking about city life
Speaking and vocabulary: Street personalities
Reading: Street life in London/Tokyo
Vocabulary 2: Phrases with *get* and *take*
Get talking and writing: Improvements in street life

Lesson 23 Gun crazy p.48
Language to go: Describing how things could have been different
Speaking and vocabulary: Crimes and criminals
Speaking and reading: *I'm sure I would have shot her*
Grammar: Third and mixed conditionals
Get talking: Situations that could have been different

Lesson 24 Difficult situations p.50
Language to go: Coping with difficult situations
Vocabulary and speaking: Phrases for describing problems
Listening: Four awkward situations
Functions: Complaining and getting results
Get talking: Roleplay: complaints

Lesson 25 Under pressure p.52

Language to go: Talking about changing situations
Vocabulary and speaking: Expressions for annoying habits
Reading: *Laughter in the workplace*
Grammar: Present continuous and present simple for describing change
Get talking: Stressful aspects of life

Lesson 26 At home p.54

Language to go: Talking about homes
Speaking and listening: Two contrasting houses
Vocabulary: Phrases to describe houses
Get talking: Your dream home

Lesson 27 A new beginning p.56

Language to go: Describing a personal change of environment
Vocabulary: US/UK English
Listening: A Pole in America
Grammar: *To be/get used to*
Get talking: A situation you had to get used to

Lesson 28 Animal magic p.58

Language to go: Describing and defining things
Speaking and reading: *Are human beings really the most advanced creatures on the planet?*
Grammar: Relative clauses
Get talking and writing: Crosswords

Lesson 29 Treat yourself p.60

Language to go: Talking about things you have done for you
Speaking and vocabulary: Expressions to describe mood
Reading and speaking: *Take it easy!*
Grammar: *To have/get something done*
Get talking: What do you have done?

Lesson 30 Growing up p.62

Language to go: Talking about growing up
Vocabulary and speaking: Ages and stages
Speaking and listening: Three people talk about important stages in their lives
Vocabulary 2: Phrasal verbs 2
Get talking and writing: Important milestones

Lesson 31 Monumental mysteries p.64

Language to go: Speculating about life in the past
Vocabulary and speaking: Word building: measurements
Reading: Machu Picchu, Stonehenge and Easter Island
Grammar: Modals for past deduction
Get talking: People in the past

Lesson 32 Film reviews p.66

Language to go: Giving your opinion
Speaking and vocabulary: Phrases for describing films
Listening: Two people's opinions on a film
Function: Expressing reactions
Get talking and writing: Film reviews

Lesson 33 Making life easier p.68

Language to go: Talking about future developments in day-to-day living
Speaking and vocabulary: Phrases to describe machines
Reading: *An easier life for the lazy generation*
Grammar: Future perfect/continuous
Get talking: Gadgets and machines

Lesson 34 In a black mood p.70

Language to go: Talking about your feelings
Speaking and vocabulary: Phrases for describing clothes
Listening: A colour therapist
Vocabulary 2: Phrases for describing emotions
Get talking: Do colours affect you?

Lesson 35 Missing the mark p.72

Language to go: Giving other people's opinions
Speaking: Predictions
Listening and vocabulary: Radio programme on erroneous predictions; verbs used for reporting
Grammar: Constructions with reporting verbs
Get talking: Reporting predictions

Lesson 36 Now or never p.74

Language to go: Telling stories
Vocabulary and speaking: Types of books
Reading: Extract from *Harley's Ghost*
Grammar: Participles in narratives
Get talking and writing: The final part of the story

Lesson 37 The dream business p.76

Language to go: Talking about working in a company
Speaking and listening: Musicmaker.com
Grammar: Prepositional phrases
Get talking and writing: Your dream company

Lesson 38 Fingers crossed p.78

Language to go: Using idiomatic English
Speaking and reading: *Seeing eye to eye with English*
Vocabulary: Body idioms
Get talking: Questions involving idioms

Lesson 39 I wish ... p.80

Language to go: Talking about regrets and missed opportunities
Speaking and vocabulary: Phrasal verbs for describing opportunities
Listening and speaking: Four missed opportunities
Grammar: *Should have/if only/wish* + past perfect
Get talking and writing: 'True Stories' radio show

Lesson 40 Mind your manners p.82

Language to go: Saying the right thing
Reading and speaking: *How polite are you?*
Listening: Social responses
Function: Using social English
Get talking: *What do you say when ...?* game

Present/future

Vocabulary 1

The past

Connecting

Verb patterns

Vocabulary 2

Modals

Functions

> Recording scripts PAGE 116   > Practice section answer key PAGE 124

Vocabulary   Phrases for talking about your life
Grammar   Review of tenses
Language to go   Talking about your job/hobby

Getting ahead

Speaking and vocabulary

1 **Look at the questions and match the phrases in *italics* with the correct definitions.**

1 Have you ever *been lucky enough to* win an award?
2 What kind of sports *are you into*?
3 What do you (hope to) do *for a living*?
4 Will learning English help you *to broaden your horizons*? How?
5 What *sacrifices* have you *made* to *achieve your goals*?
6 Do you enjoy *taking up* new hobbies? Which ones?

a) are you interested in
b) to learn about the world, through experience
c) reach your targets
d) as a job
e) had the good fortune to (do something)
f) given up something to benefit in the long term
g) starting to do/practise

2 **In pairs, answer the questions in Exercise 1.**

Listening

3 🎧 **Listen to one of the people in the photos speaking about his work. Which of them is it? What positive things does he say?**

4 **Complete these sentences from the listening. Then listen again to check.**

Example: I **believe** music is the highest form of art.

1 I first got into it when I _____ to records in my bedroom.
2 We _____ two recordings at the end of the month.
3 It _____ better than a real job.
4 At the moment, I _____ a project with some musicians in New York.
5 We _____ start touring after that.
6 I _____ able to see the world.

Grammar focus

5 Match these tenses with the sentences in Exercise 4.

Example: present simple (for habits/routines/things that are always true)
Music is the highest form of art.

1 present continuous (for things happening at the moment/temporary situations)
2 present continuous (for plans and arrangements in the future)
3 *going to* (for intentions and plans in the future)
4 past simple (for a specific time/focus in the past)
5 past continuous (for something in the past that was unfinished at a particular point)
6 present perfect (for general experience/unspecified time)

6 Look at the timeline, which represents four of the sentences from Exercise 4. Write the appropriate number in each box.

past   present   future

Practice

7 Read the text and <u>underline</u> the correct verb forms.

Robert de Niro is one of the most respected actors in Hollywood. While he *got / was getting / is getting* ready to play a part, he ¹ *is spending / spends / spent* months trying to 'get inside the head' of his character. He ² *was growing up / grew up / has grown up* in an artistic and open family and by the time he was 16, he ³ *made / has made / was making* money from acting. He made his first film, 'The Wedding Party', in 1963, but it ⁴ *wasn't / hasn't been / isn't* until 1973 that he had his big break in 'Bang the Drum Slowly'. De Niro ⁵ *made / was making / has made* over 50 films and he has also directed and produced a number of films. Some of his most famous parts include the title roles in 'The Godfather' and 'Taxi Driver'. De Niro has his own production company, Tribeca, and in future he ⁶ *is planning / planned / was planning* to focus on developing his own film projects.

Get talking ...

8 Choose something that has been important to you for a long time (for example, your job or a hobby) and draw a timeline to show how it has developed. Think about these questions.

1 How/When did you start?
2 What have you achieved so far?
3 What are you doing to develop this interest?
4 What are your future plans concerning this interest?

9 In groups, interview each member. Talk to the class about any new or interesting information you have learned about the others.

... and writing

10 Write a short text (120–180 words) about one of the members of your group, describing their career/hobby.

> GRAMMAR REFERENCE PAGE 108
> PRACTICE PAGE 88

LESSON **2**
Vocabulary

Vocabulary 1   Adjectives for describing lifestyles
Vocabulary 2   Verb phrases to describe health
Language to go   Discussing health and lifestyles

Modern survival

Speaking and vocabulary

1   Look at the photos and choose words from the box to describe the different lifestyles of the people. Explain your choices.

healthy	clean	stressful	unhealthy	exhausting
relaxing	active	polluted	stress-free	sedentary

2   a) In groups, look at these figures for life expectancy. Think about the different lifestyles in these countries (diet/work/marriage/physical and mental health/stress) and answer the questions.

Country	Men	Women
Angola	44.9	48.1
USA	72.6	79.3
Spain	73.4	80.7
Japan	75.9	81.8

(source: World Health Organisation)

1   Why do you think there are differences between the different countries?
2   Why do women live longer than men?
3   What could people do to live longer?

b) **Compare your ideas with another group.**

Listening

3   a) 〔▢▢〕 Listen to the radio interview, in which a doctor answers the questions in Exercise 2a. Make notes on what he says about the following.

- Differences between countries
- Genetics
- Marriage
- Physical and mental exercise
- Diet
- Alcohol
- Stress

b) **Compare your answers with a partner then listen again to check.**

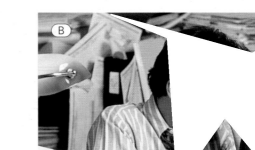

(B)

(A)

Vocabulary focus

4 Match the halves of these phrases from the first two columns, then choose the correct definition from the third column. Use the recording script on page 116 if necessary.

Example: have + a balanced diet = eat a good variety of healthy food

have	your weight	stop doing something (e.g. a habit)
watch	down on something	eat a good variety of healthy food
relieve	in good shape	pay attention to how much you weigh
be	a balanced diet	do exercise in the gym
cut	up something	become heavier
give	weight	reduce pressure
work	out	be physically fit
put on	stress	reduce the amount

D

Practice

5 Complete the sentences with expressions from Exercise 4.

Example: I've got this terrible cough. I really ought to **cut down on** the number of cigarettes I smoke.

1 I tend to eat a lot of chocolate and junk food. I don't _____ diet.
2 I try to keep fit by _____ in the gym three times a week.
3 I've put on nearly three kilos recently. I went on holiday and forgot all about _____ my _____ .
4 I've been training hard for the championship, and now I think I _____ .
5 I find that having a sauna or a massage is a wonderful way to _____ .
6 I _____ going to the gym because it was so expensive, but now I am really unfit!

Get talking ...

6 In pairs, talk about your lifestyles, using the expressions in Exercise 4.

... and writing

7 Design a poster or an information leaflet to form part of an advertising campaign for healthier lifestyles in your country.

Language to go

A: Life is so stressful nowadays.
B: I know, it's exhausting. Perhaps we should cut down on our keep-fit programme.

> PRACTICE PAGE 88

Coincidences

Vocabulary and speaking

1 **a) Choose two words or phrases from the box which could replace each word or phrase in *italics*.**

> simultaneously   earlier   afterwards   every time
> previously   subsequently   at the same time   whenever

1 Have you ever been introduced to someone but forgotten their name *later*? <u>afterwards</u> / _____
2 Are there any places which remind you of someone *each time* you go there?
3 Have you ever experienced something which you had dreamed about *before*?
4 Have you and another person ever said exactly the same thing *at the same moment*?

b) In groups, answer the questions.

Reading and speaking

2 **Read about some real-life coincidences then match these titles with the stories.**

a) **FAMILY REUNION**

b) The wrong number

c) **A SHARED HISTORY**

d) LIFE SAVER

3 **In pairs, discuss these questions.**

1 Which stories do the cartoons illustrate?
2 Which coincidence do you find most amazing?
3 Which would you describe as a) a lucky coincidence? b) a strange coincidence?

You'll never believe it!

1 John Peskett – who first met his wife Shirley when he was 21 – discovered, when she showed him her favourite childhood photo, that he and his family *had been sitting* next to her on the same Somerset beach twenty years earlier.

2 A young architect, Harold Archer, threw himself in front of a train, but was saved – an inch from death – by a passenger on the train who *pulled* the emergency handle because she 'suddenly felt she should'.

3 Londoner Charlie Crook one day decided to drive 180 km to Gloucester to visit his cousin, John Barker, whom he hadn't seen for eight years. Barker *had simultaneously decided* to drive and see Charlie – and met him halfway, where they crashed into each other.

4 Suspicious police officer Peter Moscardi, on night patrol, saw an open door, entered a factory office and decided to pick up a phone that *was ringing*. He discovered it was a friend of his calling for a chat. Moscardi had previously given him the police station phone's last four numbers incorrectly – therefore giving him the factory's telephone number.

from *ES Magazine*

Grammar focus

4 Match the phrases in *italics* in the text with the following tense descriptions, then complete the names of the remaining three tenses.

1 <u>Past continuous</u>: refers to an action that was in progress when something else happened.
2 Past _____ : refers to completed actions in the past.
3 Past _____ : refers to actions completed *before* events in the past.
4 Past _____ : refers to progressive actions that started before the main events happened in the past.

Practice

5 **Put the verbs in brackets into the correct tenses.**

Sarah Jones and Judith Thomson, from England, <u>grew up</u> (grow up) on the same street and ¹ _____ (become) best friends. Judith was Sarah's bridesmaid in 1947. Then Sarah emigrated to the USA and they ² _____ (lose) touch. Fifty-three years later, they ³ _____ (bump) into each other while they ⁴ _____ (wait) in a queue at a petrol station in Nevada, USA. They immediately ⁵ _____ (recognise) each other, even though they ⁶ _____ (not see) each other for 50 years. While they ⁷ _____ (talk), they ⁸ _____ (find out) they ⁹ _____ (live) and working on the same street in the USA for seventeen years, but ¹⁰ _____ (never see) each other.

6 🔊 **Listen to part of the text and mark the stressed words. Check your answers in the recording script on page 116, then, in pairs, take turns to read the extract aloud.**

Get talking ...

7 **Prepare to talk about five important dates in your life, and the background to those events (for example, births, marriage, graduation etc.). Make notes in the chart.**

Date and important event	Background
1999 – I bought my first house.	• *I'd been living in a friend's flat for two years. Before that I'd moved lots of times.*
2000 – I got married.	• *I'd met my boyfriend at university.*
2001 –	

8 **In groups, take turns to talk about a) the main events, then b) the background information. Tell the class about any coincidences or similarities.**

... and writing

9 **Write about the five events you chose.**

Language to go

A: What were you doing at ten o'clock last night, Mr Smith?
B: I was watching TV. I'd been out with my friends.

> GRAMMAR REFERENCE PAGE 108
> PRACTICE PAGE 89

Vocabulary   Noun combinations with -*friend* and -*mate*
Grammar   Phrases of addition, result and contrast
Language to go   Discussing advantages and disadvantages

Friends

Vocabulary and speaking

1   **Describe the different aspects of friendship illustrated in the photos.**

3   **Use words from Exercise 2 to describe the people in the photos.**

4   **Answer these questions.**

1   Think about your friends. Have you ever:
– looked after them when they were sick?
– helped them to recover from a personal crisis?
– told them a painful truth which concerned them?
– given them something that was yours?
2   Who can people turn to when they have a problem?

Listening

5   📼 **Listen to Chris Johnson talking about friendship. What does he say about:**

1   the number of close friends people have?
2   changes in friendship in the last 30 years?
3   computers and their effect on friendship?

2   **Complete the diagram with the words in the box.**

| class   fair-weather   work   pen   girl/boy |
| soul   flat   close |

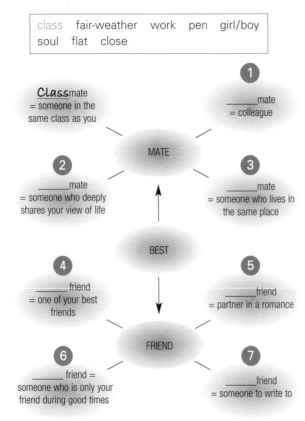

6   **Listen again and complete the sentences. Look at the recording script on page 116 to check your answers.**

Example: You'll probably only have about three close friends, **as well as** a few 'semi-detached' ones.

1   People don't think they have the time to see their friends, and _____ we don't have as many as our grandparents' generation.
2   We're busy and, _____ , we don't socialise?
3   We do [socialise]. _____ , we _____ apply the same principles to friendship as we do to anything else in life.
4   '... you could be finishing a report for work or in the gym getting fit?'
'_____ , why bother going to the gym when you could be spending time with friends?'
5   _____ you'd have thought that, with modern-day means of communication, it's easier to keep in touch with people.
6   'It's easier to keep in touch with people.'
'Yes, but _____ , something like the Internet doesn't really bond people, does it?'

Practice

9 Read the text and <u>underline</u> the correct alternative.

The Samaritans: The Friends at the End of the Line

The Samaritans was founded in 1953 by a vicar called Chad Varah. Varah thought people often needed someone to listen to their problems, and that this kind of therapy could *too* / *also* / *however* help to save lives. At first, Varah worked alone. ¹ *However* / *As well as* / *On the other hand*, he soon realised he needed help. ² *Although* / *Also* / *As a result* he set up an office for volunteers. He decided 'listeners' should be available all day, and at night ³ *also* / *too* / *nevertheless*. Their help would be confidential and unprejudiced. ⁴ *Because of this* / *Although* / *Also* the Samaritans couldn't give their own opinions concerning politics or religion. ⁵ *On the other hand* / *Although* / *However* the Samaritans work long hours and in shifts, they are not paid. Seventy-one per cent of the volunteers are female, and on average a volunteer takes 262 calls a year. ⁶ *Although* / *However* / *Also*, no one will ever know how many lives they have saved.

Get talking ...

10 In groups, prepare to discuss the pros (good points) and cons (bad points) of these situations.

Group A: discuss and make notes on the pros of the situation.
Group B: discuss and make notes on the cons of the situation.

- Making friends on the Internet
- Having famous friends
- Having friends to stay in your house
- Having friends who do the same job as you

In pairs, discuss the situations and draw conclusions. Try to use the expressions in Exercise 7 to link your ideas.

... and writing

11 Choose one of the situations and write an article discussing the pros and cons (150 words).

Grammar focus

7 **Put these linking words and phrases under the correct headings.**

> because of this   as a result   on the other hand
> although   nevertheless   also   as well as
> however   therefore   too

Contrast	Result	Addition
nevertheless	because of this	too

8 **Answer these questions.**

1 Which link of contrast never goes at the end of a sentence?
2 Which link of result is the most formal?
3 Which link of addition can go at the end of a sentence?

Language to go

A: It's good to have penfriends and to make friends on the Internet too.
B: Yes, but on the other hand, it's not the same as having friends in the flesh.

> GRAMMAR REFERENCE PAGE 108
> PRACTICE PAGE 89

Vocabulary   Ways of talking
Grammar   Question tags
Language to go   Making small talk at a party

Small talk

Vocabulary and speaking

1   **In pairs, talk about the picture. What do you think the people are saying? How are they feeling?**

2   **Match the sentences with a verb from the box which describes what the speakers are saying or doing.**

> gossip   chat   confide in   moan about
> make small talk   shout

1   'I'll tell you a secret, but you won't tell anyone else, will you?'
2   'Hey! Andy! We're over here!'
3   'Anyway, she said to him, "I know you know", and he said, "What do you know?"'
4   'Mmm, lovely food! Have you been to one of these parties before?'
5   'I don't know what to do about him. He never rings me back, and he's always late …'
6   'I really needed this coffee break. Hey, have you seen what's on TV tonight?'

3   **In pairs, use some of the verbs in Exercise 2 to describe what the people in the picture are doing. When do *you* talk in these ways?**

Reading

4   **Read the article and add *do* or *don't* to each tip.**

Example: *1 Do chat about holidays and free time.*

Conversation stunners

Have you ever been to a party and found you have nothing to say? Try these top tips.

1   Chat about holidays and free time – something we all have in common.
2   Make sure you know who you are confiding in, especially if you're gossiping or criticising someone.
3   Leave without inviting someone out.
4   Bore people by moaning about your nightmare journey.
5   Make small talk. Read newspapers and watch the news. If you don't have time for books and films, read the reviews.
6   Count to four in your head before interrupting someone. Otherwise it sounds like you couldn't wait for the other person to shut up.
7   Get into deep conversations about your life story.

Listening

5 🔊 Listen to the conversations and match them with the advice in Exercise 4.

Example: *Example conversation + Advice 1*

6 Listen again and complete the sentences.

Example: The weather's been lovely, *hasn't it?* What did you get up to over the weekend?

1 A: We had terrible trouble getting here.
   B: Really? It doesn't usually take long, _____ ?
   A: No, but first we were delayed, and then the train was cancelled.
2 A: It was a fantastic film, _____ ?
   B: Yes. Brilliant.
   C: Really? I haven't seen it yet.
   B: Oh, you must. Let's go together, _____ ?
3 A: I mean, you can't seriously call that art, _____ ? It's so ugly, _____ ? You're not the artist, _____ ?
   B: Actually it's a fake. You won't tell anyone, _____ ?
4 A: Times have changed, _____ ? Life was very different then. When I was a boy we used to …
   B: Excuse me a moment.'
5 A: See you at the exhibition on Sunday. You will be there, _____ ?
   B: I can't wait.

Grammar focus

7 Look at these examples from Exercise 5 and explain how question tags are formed. Question tags are used to …

check information: 'It doesn't usually take long, *does it?*'

ask for agreement: 'It was a fantastic film, *wasn't it?*'

8 Listen to the conversations from Exercise 5 again. Are they checking information or asking for agreement? Mark the tags with an arrow.

Practice

9 Write question tags to complete the following statements.

Example: He's gorgeous, *isn't he?*

1 It's been fantastic weather, _____ ?
2 It was an awful journey, _____ ?
3 She made all this food herself, _____ ?
4 There isn't any more wine, _____ ?
5 You don't happen to know where the toilet is, _____ ?
6 She could have rung to say she wasn't coming, _____ ?
7 You will stay for dinner, _____ ?
8 They can't have forgotten, _____ ?
9 You work in computers, _____ ?

10 🔊 Listen to check your answers. Notice how the other speaker responds. Then practise saying the sentences.

Get talking

11 Imagine you are going to have a party. Write the names of your classmates and the topics you want to ask them about.

Names	Information
Marco	married?
Gill	holiday next week?
Robert	just finished university?

Walk around the room asking the questions, using tags.

Language to go

A: This is a great party, isn't it?
B: Yes! You didn't come to the last one, did you?

> GRAMMAR REFERENCE PAGE 109
> PRACTICE PAGE 90

LESSON **6**
Vocabulary

Vocabulary 1 Expressions for describing relationships
Vocabulary 2 Phrasal verbs 1
Language to go Talking about a relationship

True love

Vocabulary and speaking

1 Match the verbs on the left with the phrases on the right. Find as many different combinations as you can.

last	in love
have	together
fall	a long time
get	a lot in common
be	divorced
work	a happy marriage
spend	in the public eye
	time apart

2 Answer these questions.

1 What is the difference between *to be ...* and *to get ...*?
2 Which verb can mean *to become*?
3 Which verb can describe a state?

3 Look at the photos and say what you know about these couples. If possible, use the expressions in Exercise 1.

Reading and speaking

4 a) In pairs, read your texts and complete the table. If you aren't sure, write ?.

Student A: Turn to page 84.
Student B: Turn to page 86.

b) Share information with your partner to complete the table.

Couple	How did they meet?	What were the most important things that happened during their relationship?	Why did the relationship finish?
Nelson and Winnie Mandela			
Richard Burton and Liz Taylor			

Winnie and Nelson Mandela

Richard Burton and Liz Taylor

Vocabulary focus

5 In groups, choose the best definition for each phrasal verb in *italics*.

Example: They got divorced. However, they *made up*.
a) became friends again after an argument ✔
b) started to live together

1 They *got back together* and remarried.
  a) started a relationship
  b) resumed a relationship
2 Winnie and Nelson *fell out* over political and personal differences.
  a) had an argument
  b) moved house
3 Winnie and Nelson *split up*.
  a) remarried   b) separated
4 Winnie first *came across* Nelson Mandela … in a law court.
  a) met by chance
  b) arranged to meet
5 Burton and Taylor couldn't *get over* the problems …
  a) recover from something or return to normal
  b) improve something
6 Burton and Taylor *got on* well.
  a) started living together
  b) had a friendly relationship

6 Look at the examples and say which phrasal verb is transitive (must have an object) and which is intransitive (doesn't have an object).

1 Winnie first *came across* Nelson …
2 Winnie and Nelson *fell out*.

Which type is each verb in Exercise 5?

Practice

7 🔲 In pairs, complete the text using the phrasal verbs in Exercise 5, then listen to check your answers.

Marilyn Monroe, one of the cinema's most famous faces, married her first husband when she was sixteen, but they didn't <u>get on</u> and, four years later, they got divorced. In 1954, she married the baseball star, Joe DiMaggio. They ¹ _____ frequently, though, and separated. The following year, she ² _____ Arthur Miller while she was in New York. After a five-year marriage, they too ³ _____ . In 1962, she ⁴ _____ with DiMaggio and they ⁵ _____ together. They were planning to get married again, but she died after taking an overdose of sleeping pills. Monroe entertained millions of people but never found lasting happiness. Some say she never ⁶ _____ the problems of her lonely childhood.

8 🔲 Listen to the phrasal verbs from Exercise 7 and mark the stress. Where is the main stress usually found?

Get talking …

9 In pairs, look at these pictures and tell the story.

… and writing

10 Write the story, using the phrasal verbs.

> GRAMMAR REFERENCE PAGE 109
> PRACTICE PAGE 90

Vocabulary   Phrases to describe behaviour
Grammar   Obligation verbs
Language to go   Discussing ways of bringing up children

Ⓑ

The daddy of discipline

Vocabulary and speaking

1   **Find pairs of expressions in the box which have similar meanings.**

Example: playing truant/
taking time off school (without
permission)

> playing truant   doing chores
> doing odd jobs in the house
> getting into trouble
> doing what you're told   obeying
> taking time off school (without
> permission)
> being naughty (and getting caught)

2   **Use the expressions from Exercise 1 to describe what the children in the photos are doing.**

3   **In groups, discuss the following.**

1   What types of things do parents and children have conflicts about?
2   What rules did your parents make when you were a child?
3   Do you think parents are more or less strict nowadays?

Reading

4   **Read the article about John Rosemond's views on bringing up children and answer the questions.**

1   How does he believe parents have changed their behaviour?
2   What does he think they should do now?

5   **In pairs, look at Rosemond's commandments again and discuss which ones you agree with.**

Ⓐ

Seven ways to be a good parent

A whole new wave of tough parenting is setting a revolutionary agenda in childcare on both sides of the Atlantic.

Writing in more than 150 newspapers and selling more than three million copies of his books, John Rosemond and his ideas could have a huge influence on the next generation of American children. Why and how?

Here are his seven commandments:

1   You should pay more attention to your marriage than to your children.

2   Expect your children to obey, and punish them every time they don't.

3   In order to build up their characters, you must make them do lots of chores.

4   Give them regular and realistic doses of 'Vitamin N'. (Say No.)

5   You mustn't let them have too many toys.

6   Limit their dependence on television.

7   Stop trying to make them happy all the time, and stop trying to be popular with them. You don't

Grammar focus

6 Look at these phrases from the article and answer the questions.

1 *should* vs *ought to*
- You *should pay* more attention to your marriage.
- You *should show* your love for them.

Can you replace the modal *should* with *ought to* in these sentences?

2 *don't have to* vs *mustn't/needn't*
- You *don't have to buy* presents.

Can you replace this verb with *mustn't* or *needn't*?
Does this change the meaning? How?

3 *are supposed to* vs *need to*
- ... what they *are supposed to do*.

Can you replace the verb here with *need to*?

7 Put the verbs above into four groups: obligation, lack of obligation, prohibition, advice/suggestions.

have to buy endless presents as a sign of your affection. Instead, you should show your love for them by doing what you have to do to turn them into decent, law-abiding citizens.

These views stem from Rosemond's central belief: American parents have become too weak, and they need to reclaim their authority. He sees a country full of parents being ruled by their children, who are allowed to do what they want when they want to, and who don't know the meaning of the word 'no'. And Rosemond doesn't like what he sees. He believes in parent power.

Once he was a long-haired, drug-taking rebel. But then he got married, had a child and grew up. He says that because of theories in child development, parents are now confused and unsure of what they are supposed to do. He says parents shouldn't worry. They ought to go back to basics – quick, easy and theory-free.

The truth is that Rosemond is an anti-expert childcare expert. He thinks parents have to take back the control they once had over their kids; to be free of the experts and the theory-makers. And if America swallows his ideas, who knows? Perhaps the next generation will grow up more disciplined than the last, and maybe their parents will get the respect they deserve.

from *The Observer* newspaper

Practice

8 📼 Rephrase the sentences using the verbs from Exercise 6, then listen to the recording for some possible answers.

Example: I've got my exams next week. I really need to revise.
I really ought to revise for my exams next week.

1 It's not necessary to wear uniforms at school.
We ...
2 If you want to help your mother, it's a good idea to wash the dishes.
You ...
3 There is no need for her to worry about us. We'll be fine.
She ...
4 It wouldn't be a good idea to take the car without asking him first.
You ...
5 My mother is always telling me not to eat so much junk food.
I ...
6 Don't speak to any strangers in the street.
You ...

9 Listen to the phrases again and repeat them. What happens to the words *to*, *should* and *not* in the sentences? Are they stressed?

Get talking

10 In groups, discuss the following question, then present your ideas to the rest of the class.

What do you feel children should and shouldn't be allowed to do? Decide on seven commandments. Think about study/food/bed times/ free time/household responsibilities/ play/school.

Language to go

A: Children ought to watch less TV.
B: And they shouldn't get into trouble so often.

> GRAMMAR REFERENCE PAGE 109
> PRACTICE PAGE 91

Vocabulary   Humour
Functions   Agreeing, disagreeing, giving and asking for opinions
Language to go   Discussing what makes you laugh

That's funny

Speaking and vocabulary

1   Look at the photos and answer the questions.

  1   Do you know either of these comedians?
  2   Have you ever seen them on TV?
  3   Which other famous comedians can you think of?

2   Match the contrasting phrases with their definitions.

  1   a person telling a joke / a person getting a joke
  2   a stand-up comedian / a sitcom
  3   to find something funny / to have fun
  4   verbal humour / visual humour
  5   to make someone laugh / to have the last laugh

  a)   to be so amused that you laugh / to enjoy yourself, generally
  b)   to cause another person to laugh / what you have when you've finally been successful or won an argument
  c)   someone who stands up on a stage, making the audience laugh / a funny TV series with the same characters every week
  d)   someone who tells a funny story / someone who laughs because he/she understands it
  e)   something that is funny because of the words / something that is funny because of what you see

Listening

3   📖 Listen to four conversations answering the question 'What's funny?' Look at the table below and tick (✔) the things that make these people laugh. Put a cross (✗) for the things they don't find funny.

person	physical humour	people telling jokes	people making mistakes	film/TV	irony	comedians imitating famous people	cartoons
Amanda (UK)							
Johnny (USA)							
Pablo (Argentina)							
Jeanne (France)							

Language focus

4 **Write these expressions in the table according to their function.**

Absolutely!	I suppose …
Do you really think so?	I think …
Exactly!	I'd go along with that.
For me …	I'd have to agree with you.
From my point of view, …	I'm not sure about that.
How about you?	In my view …
I disagree.	Personally, …
I know what you mean.	Right.
I reckon …	What about …?
I see what you mean.	What do you think of …?

Agreeing	Disagreeing
I know what you mean.	
Giving an opinion	Asking for an opinion

5 🔲 **Mark where the stress falls in each phrase, then listen to check.**

Example: absolutely

Practice

6 **Complete these dialogues using phrases from Exercise 4.**

Example: A: I think Mr Bean is the best comedian ever.
B: **I'm not sure about that.**

1 A: Laughter or crying is what a human being does when there's nothing else he can do.
  B: I'd go _____ .
2 A: Comedy is medicine.
  B: I know _____ .
3 A: What _____ Woody Allen's films?
  B: In _____ , they're very funny.
  A: Do you _____ so?
4 A: From my _____ , it's not the joke that's funny. It's the way you tell it. How _____ ?
  B: _____ !
5 A: I _____ comedy is a funny way of being serious. What _____ ?
  B: I'd _____ agree _____ .

7 🔲 **Listen to check, paying attention to the intonation. In pairs, take turns to read the dialogues aloud.**

Get talking

8 **In groups, discuss what type of humour you like. Look at the photos for ideas.**

Language to go

A: In my view, clowns are very funny.
B: I'd go along with that.

> GRAMMAR REFERENCE PAGE 110
> PRACTICE PAGE 91

Vocabulary   Weekend activities
Grammar   Tenses for describing future plans
Language to go   Making plans

A perfect weekend

Vocabulary and speaking

1   Look at the photo. Do you ever go to cafés like this?

2   a) In pairs, look at the phrases in the box.

> have a lie-in
> do some window-shopping
> get some exercise
> catch up with friends
> surf the Net   stay in
> do some DIY
> do the housework   go clubbing
> (sit in a café and) do some
> people-watching

Which of those activities would you do …?

Example: in bed   *have a lie-in*

1   in the gym
2   if your flat was a mess
3   if you enjoyed looking at other people
4   if you liked buying things but were short of money
5   to find out new information quickly
6   if you liked loud music
7   if you had been out of touch
8   if you were too tired to socialise
9   if you liked making things with your hands

b) **Talk about how many of these activities you enjoy doing and when you do them.**

Reading

3   **Read Tina and Ben's e-mails and put them in the correct order.**

Example: *A, …*

A

Hi there,
I hope all's well with you, and that you've had a good week. I've heard the weather's going to be beautiful at the weekend. Do you fancy doing something? It would be nice to catch up.
Ben

B

Great! By the way, what are you doing tonight? I'm staying in for a change.
B

C

Nothing too energetic – it's been a long, hard week. I'm having a lie-in on Saturday – that's definite. But I wouldn't mind going for a picnic in the park. Or we could go and see a film. The new Tom Cruise film is opening at The Ritzy. It starts at 6.00. How about a late lunch in the park followed by the cinema? Then maybe a drink?
B

D

Good idea. Actually, I don't know if you're interested, but there's an art exhibition on at the Tate Gallery. It's by a modern artist, and I can't remember her name! But it's supposed to be very good. Maybe you'd like to go with me in the afternoon.
T

E

Yes, it would. I'm going to meet my cousin on Saturday morning – we're going window-shopping, but after that I'm free. What have you got in mind?
Tina

F

I'll call you on Saturday morning to arrange a time. Not too early!
T

G

Sleeping! Speak to you Saturday.
T

H

Modern art? Errr … !! OK, but I'm warning you now – I won't understand any of it. But I'll come along anyway. When shall we meet?
B

4   **Describe their final plans for the weekend.**

Practice

6 Underline the correct verb.

Example: I've decided. *I'm going to learn / I'll learn / I'm learning* to speak French.

1 You've dropped your pen. *I'll pick it up / I'm going to pick it up / I'm picking it up* for you.
2 Next Christmas? *We'll visit / We're visiting / We visit* my grandmother for the first time in years. She's really looking forward to it.
3 One great Scottish event which happens every summer is the Edinburgh Festival. It *will start / is starting / starts* at the end of July and *will finish / is finishing / finishes* in August.
4 I know why she has been so happy. She *will get / is getting / get* married next month.
5 Oh, no! It's Dad's birthday today and I forgot to send him a card! *I'll call / I'm going to call / I'm calling* him later.
6 *I will meet / I'm meeting / I meet* Jim this evening, and we're going out for a meal, if you want to join us.
7 *Are you coming / Do you come / Will you be* to Tania's party on Saturday?

Get talking ...

7 Arrange a day trip for yourself and two or three other students. Think about:

- where to go/what to do
- where/what to eat
- how to travel
- time/place to meet

... and writing

8 Make the arrangements by writing short notes or e-mails like Tina and Ben's.

Example: Hi Marco, What are you up to on Saturday?
Marcia and I are thinking of ...

Grammar focus

5 Look at the sentences from the e-mails and complete the rules using the words in the box.

> The present simple
> The present continuous
> *Going to* + infinitive
> *Will*

1 The weather*'s going to be* beautiful.
  <u>Going to + infinitive</u> is used to describe intentions OR predictions based on present evidence.
2 I*'m having* a lie-in on Saturday.
  _____ is used to describe planned events and arrangements.
3 It [the film] *starts* at 6.00.
  _____ can be used to describe fixed future events, e.g. programmes and timetables.
4 I*'ll give* you a call on Saturday morning.
  _____ can be used to make a spontaneous decision in reaction to a present situation.

Language to go

A: Do you fancy doing **something exciting at the weekend?**
B: I can't. I'm visiting my grandmother.

> GRAMMAR REFERENCE PAGE 110
> PRACTICE PAGE 92

Vocabulary   Expressions for describing yourself, your skills and experience
Language to go   Writing a CV

Just the job

Speaking and reading

CV /si: 'vi:/ also **curriculum vitae** *n* [C] *BrE* a
document that describes your education and the jobs
you have done, used when you are trying to get a
new job; résumé *AmE*

from *Longman Dictionary of Contemporary English*

1   **In pairs, answer the questions.**

1   Have you got an up-to-date CV?
2   What is important to remember when writing your CV?
3   How long should the ideal CV be?

2   **Read the text and find the answers to Questions 2 and 3 in Exercise 1.**

GETTING YOUR FOOT IN THE DOOR

How to write an effective CV

- **Make sure your skills, interests and work experience match the job exactly.**

- **Put your education and career in reverse order (the most recent first).**

- **Don't leave unexplained gaps in your career.**

- **Don't lie, or you may be caught out in the interview. Go back through your jobs and assignments to identify tasks, responsibilities and particularly accomplishments.**

- **Use positive language to talk about your achievements and skills: expressions like 'successfully co-ordinated' and 'took responsibility for'.**

- **Give names, addresses, phone numbers and e-mail addresses of at least two people who can give a reference, i.e. say that you were a good employee or student.**

- **Print onto one side of a single sheet of good-quality A4 paper.**

3   **Decide whether you agree with the advice in the text.**

4   **Read the job advertisement and the CV. In pairs, discuss these questions.**

1   Does the CV follow the advice in the text?
2   How could it be improved?
3   Would Charlie Thompson be a good candidate for this job?

Vocabulary focus

5   **Match the phrases in *italics* in the CV with the following definitions.**

Example: pays attention to detail
has a good eye for detail

1   good at talking to people
2   improved by working on
3   has lots of experience
4   encouraging
5   has a mature, responsible attitude
6   organised
7   can show that he's worked successfully in management
8   was the leader of
9   is organised

6   **Put each of the phrases from Exercise 5 into one of the following categories.**

- Expressions to describe yourself
- Expressions to describe your work skills
- Expressions to describe your achievements

Charlie Thompson
12 Rayners Gardens, Ruislip, Middlesex TW3 9HP
tel: 020 8557 3590 e-mail: cthompson@mail.com

CV

PROFILE
- An innovative and *highly experienced* Development Researcher with *proven managerial skills*.

PERSONAL DETAILS
- Male
- Date of birth: 30.5.74

TRAINING AND QUALIFICATIONS
1984–1992	Stoke School, Buckingham. 3 'A' levels (B, B, C)
1992–1995	University of Exeter, BA Honours in Sociology (2.2)
1995–1997	London Media School, Diploma in Film Studies

EXPERIENCE
2001–present	Development Researcher/Programmer, Yoonie TV
1998–1999	Associate Producer for the Mediaworld Breakfast Show
1997–1998	Researcher/producer, Transworld Sport TV

ACHIEVEMENTS
- Has successfully researched and *developed* a range of TV programmes for Open University education.
- Designed and *co-ordinated* the new weekend schedule for Yoonie TV.
- *Ran* an initiative for Yoonie TV to introduce new medias into the programming schedule.

PROFESSIONAL QUALITIES
- Skilful at developing and *motivating* teams to achieve their objectives.
- Able to work on own initiative and as part of a team.
- *Excellent communication skills.*
- *Professional. Good organisational skills and has a good eye for detail.*

OTHER SKILLS AND INTERESTS
IT skills, speaks French and Spanish fluently, well travelled, other interests include sailing and skiing

REFERENCES
Mr J.D. Smythe	Ms N. Wilkins,
Transworld Sport	Yoonie TV
PO Box 38	29 Edgar Street
London NW1 9YY	Buckingham B3 2CW
jdsmythe@transworld.com	01333 779933

MBC WORLDWIDE
Programme Development Researcher

Due to expansion in the MBC Worldwide Channel for Students, opportunities have arisen for a number of senior positions.

We are looking for an experienced Programme Development Researcher to develop and implement our new programme schedule for Language Students.

If you are a creative and motivated researcher with a proven background in Programme Development, contact Jean for further details.

Practice

7   In groups, discuss what requirements or skills are necessary for the jobs in the photos. Would you like to do any of the jobs? Do you have any of the necessary skills?

Get writing

8   Decide what job you would like to apply for (choose one of the photos or any other job). Plan and write your CV.

football coach
politician
architect

Language to go

A: Your profile says you are unable to work as part of a team, and lack good communication and organisational skills.
B: Yes, I'm looking for a job in management.

> PRACTICE PAGE 92

11
The past

Vocabulary   The media
Grammar   Present perfect: simple/continuous
Language to go   Having a job interview and talking about your experience

In the media

Vocabulary and speaking

1   **In pairs, look at the TV programme types and answer the questions.**

> soap opera   documentary   nature programme
> feature film   series   chat show   comedy show
> quiz show   advert   drama   thriller
> sports programme   music channel/show
> cartoon   children's programme

1   Which programmes can you see in the photos?
2   Which programmes do you enjoy watching?
3   Which programmes do you think could be useful for students learning English?
4   Which types of programme can you watch, in English, in your country?

2   **Look at the job advertised on page 23 which Charlie has applied for. In pairs, discuss what sort of experience you think he needs.**

Listening

3   **a)**  **Listen to Charlie answering the following questions in the interview and number them in the order he answers them.**

- ☐ How do you feel that your experience would help you in this position?
- ☐ What has brought about this change?
- ☐ Tell me about yourself and why you applied for the job.
- ☐ What have you learnt from this experience?
- ☐ What do you feel that you, in particular, have to offer the company?
- ☐ Tell me about your current position. What exactly have you been doing?

b) Check your answers in pairs. What is his answer to each question?

4    **Listen to two extracts from the interview again. Underline the correct tenses.**

C: I've always *enjoyed* / *been enjoying* TV … I've ¹ *worked* / *been working* in Programme Development for about five years now, and recently I've ² *looked* / *been looking* for a new challenge …

I: What has ³ *brought* / *been bringing* about this change?

C: I've ⁴ *worked* / *been working* for a few different television companies now and I feel ready for the next step.

I: Could you tell me a bit more about your current position and exactly what you have ⁵ *done* / *been doing*?

C: Yes, I've ⁶ *worked* / *been working* for a university TV channel called Yoonie TV.

* * *

C: Well, I've ⁷ *worked* / *been working* on a variety of programme types, as you can see from my CV. I've ⁸ *developed* / *been developing* documentaries, and ⁹ *researched* / *been researching* topics for student debate shows, ¹⁰ *worked* / *been working* on breakfast chat shows, and ¹¹ *prepared* / *been preparing* sports interviews. Basically, I've ¹² *been involved* / *been being involved* in creating shows for all genres, on different networks.

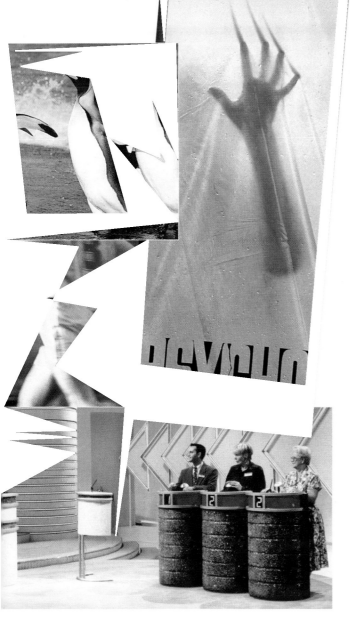

Grammar focus

5 **In pairs, look at the examples and answer the questions.**

1 Are both the following sentences grammatically correct?
- I**'ve worked** in Programme Development for about five years now.
- I**'ve been working** in Programme Development for about five years now.

2 Does the different tense change the meaning in this example?

3 In which of the following sentences is Charlie talking about completed events?
- I**'ve been working** for a university TV channel called Yoonie TV.
- I**'ve worked** on a variety of programme types, as you can see from my CV.

6 **Look at your answers to Exercise 4 and discuss why you chose each tense.**

7 🔲 **Listen to the sentences from Exercise 5. How are *have* and *been* pronounced? Repeat the sentences, copying the pronunciation.**

Practice

8 **Read the dialogues and <u>underline</u> the correct tenses, then practise saying the dialogues in pairs.**

Example: A: What on earth have you *done* / *been doing*? You're filthy!
B: I've *fixed* / *been fixing* the car.

1 A: I've *been looking* / *looked* for you all morning. Have you *spoken* / *been speaking* to Michael yet?
B: No, I haven't *had* / *been having* time.

2 A: It's very quiet in here. What is everybody up to?
B: Oh, they've *played* / *been playing* computer games all afternoon.

3 A: Have you *heard* / *been hearing* the news?
B: About the bomb? Yes. They've just *arrested* / *been arresting* two suspects.

4 A: Hi. I haven't *seen* / *been seeing* you for ages. What have you *done* / *been doing*?
B: Nothing interesting. I have *worked* / *been working* too hard.

5 A: Have you *seen* / *been seeing* my car keys anywhere?
B: No. You haven't *lost* / *been losing* them again, have you?

6 A: Have you *finished* / *been finishing* your exams yet?
B: Yes, and I've *passed* / *been passing* them all!

Get talking

9 **Prepare to talk about your work experience in a job interview by answering the following questions.**

1 Tell me about yourself / why you have applied for this job.
2 Tell me about your current occupation, and what you have been doing recently.
3 How do you think that your previous (work) experience could help you in this position?
4 What do you feel you, in particular, have to offer?

10 **In pairs, say which job you have chosen. Interview each other using the questions above and any others you wish to ask. Would you give your partner the job? Why/Why not?**

Language to go

A: Have you had your interview yet?
B: No, I've been waiting for them to call.

> GRAMMAR REFERENCE PAGE 110
> PRACTICE PAGE 93

Vocabulary   Preparing and cooking food
Grammar   Countable/uncountable nouns and quantifiers
Language to go   Describing how to make a dish

Ready to cook!

Speaking and vocabulary

1   In pairs, discuss the following questions.

1   How often do you cook?
2   Have you ever cooked for eight (or more) people?
3   What's your favourite type of food?
4   What other nationalities' food is available where you live?

2   Match the words in the box with their definitions.

chop   simmer   serve   melt
(bring to the) boil   mix   add
stir   fry   roast   grill   pour

1   present a finished meal, ready for eating
2   cook in hot fat
3   turn hard food into liquid by heating it
4   put one ingredient in with another
5   cook in very hot, bubbling liquid
6   cook for a short time under strong heat
7   cut into pieces
8   blend different ingredients together
9   cook (especially meat) for a long time in the oven
10   move a spoon around in liquid while cooking
11   cook liquid gently
12   transfer liquid from a container

3   Look at pictures 1A and 2A. Match the names of the ingredients with their pictures.

Recipe 1

shrimps   butter   stock   beer
onions   salt   pepper   basil

Recipe 2

kidney beans   minced beef
vegetable oil   onions
garlic   chilli powder
tomato purée   tomatoes

Listening and speaking

4 🎧 **Listen to the ingredients needed for two recipes. Tick (✔) the picture (A or B) which shows the correct ingredients for each recipe.**

5 🎧 **Listen to the recipes and complete the sentences.**

Cajun shrimp

Example: Heat <u>about two litres of</u> water in a pan.

1 Let the stock simmer for _____ .
2 Melt _____ in a large saucepan.
3 Cook the shrimps for _____ minutes, before adding the rest of the butter.
4 Add the rest of the butter and _____ .
5 Serve with _____ .

Chilli con carne

6 Boil the kidney beans for _____ .
7 Cook the meat and onions until _____ .
8 Add the tomato purée, the _____ and the kidney beans.
9 Let the chilli con carne simmer for _____ .
10 Serve with _____ .

6 **In pairs, discuss the following questions.**

1 Have you tried either of these dishes? Would you cook either of them for guests?
2 Does either sound like a recipe from your country?

7 **Look at these phrases from the recipes and underline the correct alternatives.**

Cajun shrimp

Example: *several* / *most of* onions

1 *a few* / *a little* herbs
2 *all* / *each* the onions
3 *a little* / *a few* salt and pepper
4 *every few* / *each* minutes
5 *almost all* / *many* of the butter

Chilli con carne

6 *a little* / *a few* vegetable oil
7 *some* / *several* chilli powder
8 *a bit of* / *some of* oil
9 *a small amount of* / *a small number of* chilli powder
10 *not too much* / *not too many* oil
11 *not a great deal of* / *not a large number of* chilli powder

Grammar focus

8 **Put the words in *italics* from Exercise 7 into the correct column.**

countable	uncountable	countable or uncountable
a few	a little	

Practice

9 **Underline the correct alternatives.**

GREAT BRITISH FOOD

<u>Many</u> / *Much* tourists, on coming to Britain, complain about the food. 'Why are there so [1] *little* / *a few* / *few* restaurants which serve British food?' they say. 'Why do the British eat potatoes with [2] *all* / *every* meal?' And, 'Isn't the food [3] *a little* / *little* / *a few* expensive, considering the quality?'

Well, these questions can be answered easily. There are a large [4] *number* / *amount* of foreign restaurants in Britain because Britain is a diverse and cosmopolitan place. People enjoy food from all over the world, particularly Indian, Chinese, Italian and French. Britain's climate, which has [5] *a large number of* / *a great deal of* / *several* rain and a short summer, is good for growing vegetables, especially potatoes, so [6] *much* / *many* dishes are based on this versatile vegetable. As for the price of food, it's true Britain has a great [7] *number* / *amount* of expensive restaurants and delicatessens, but if you look carefully enough, you can find [8] *a great deal* / *lots of* cheaper places. Also, there are [9] *few* / *a few* pubs these days which don't serve hot, inexpensive food, and often it's real British food, too, like sausages and chips or shepherd's pie!

Get talking

10 **Think of a dish that you know how to cook. Make notes on ingredients and procedure. Then explain how to make your dish to a partner.**

Language to go

A: What will I need to make this dish?
B: Several large eggs, some butter, a bit of garlic and a little salt.

> GRAMMAR REFERENCE PAGE 110
> PRACTICE PAGE 93

Vocabulary   Expressions to describe gestures
Grammar   The -*ing* form / infinitive
Language to go   Discussing social behaviour

13
Verb patterns

Contact

⑤
①
②
③
④

Speaking and vocabulary

1   Match the gestures with their meanings in Britain.

1 shrug your shoulders	a) 'Hello, good to meet you.'
2 kiss someone on the cheek	b) 'I don't know.'
3 pat someone on the back	c) 'Good luck.'
4 wave	d) 'That one, please.'
5 point at something	e) 'Nice to see you again.'
6 shake hands	f) 'I'm joking.'
7 wink	g) 'Well done.'
8 cross your fingers	h) 'Goodbye.'

2   In pairs, say what the people in the pictures are doing. Use the expressions from Exercise 1.

3   Answer these questions.

1   Do the gestures mean the same in your country?
2   When do you use them?
3   Can you think of any others you use?

4   In pairs, discuss these statements about the British and kissing. Which ones do you think are true?

1   Most Britons think social kissing is embarrassing.
2   British people are happy to kiss a new acquaintance.
3   Kissing relatives and friends is common in Britain.
4   The British think that kissing a lot shows a warm personality.

Reading

5   Read the article and check your answers to Exercise 4.

6   In pairs, discuss whether you agree with the article.

Why Britain suffers a kissing crisis

It's a dilemma for every British socialite – do you kiss the host or shake hands?

One in four Britons *fails to* see the point of social kissing and *continues to* think it is embarrassing. Sixty per cent would *choose to* just shake hands, and one in three thinks that social kissing is about '*pretending*' *to* be friendly.

Just one in ten Britons positively approve of kissing a new acquaintance; many see it as 'un-British' and *avoid touching* at all if possible.

Fifty-one per cent of us *suggest kissing* women is OK, but *admit being* suspicious of kissing between men, and most people would *attempt to* pull away if someone they did not know well *tried to* kiss them. They would also *refuse to* return an unexpected or unwanted kiss.

As you might *expect to* find, in close relationships nearly all of us kiss our relatives and 80 per cent of us *manage to* kiss our closest friends. But, according to psychologist Oliver James, when we British kiss virtual strangers, it has nothing to do with *wanting to* spread a little happiness, and rarely has the genuine warmth of the Italians or the Spanish. In fact, people actually *resent having* to put up with physical contact.

'When we *go around kissing* people we don't know very well, we're really just desperately *attempting to* get close. *Remember to* be careful: big kissers aren't necessarily warm and giving – they may just be lonely.'

from *Metro* newspaper

Practice

9 **Complete the sentences with a verb from each box, in the correct form.**

Example: I don't choose <u>to do</u> the housework. I resent <u>having</u> to do it at all!

| tip | get | point |
| do | see | take |

| arrive | have | ask |
| touch | eat | get |

1 I fail _____ what's so strange about _____ dinner at five o'clock.
2 Remember _____ the hotel porter if you want _____ good service again!
3 You can't expect _____ much help by _____ police officers for directions.
4 If someone invites you to their house for dinner, you should probably try _____ a bottle of wine and remember _____ about ten minutes late.
5 If you travel in Asia, you should avoid _____ at or _____ people's heads.

10 In pairs, discuss the statements in Exercise 9.

Grammar focus

7 **a) Match the sentences with the rules.**

1 They would *refuse to return* an unwanted kiss.
2 When we *go around kissing* people we don't know …
3 The British *avoid touching*.

a) Some verbs are followed by the the the *-ing* form.
b) Some verbs are followed by the infinitive with *to*.
c) Prepositions are generally followed by the *-ing* form.

b) Look at these two sentences and say whether there is a difference in meaning. Then complete the rule.

1 Remember to lock the door.
2 I remember locking the door.

Some verbs may be followed by the _____ form or the _____ , with a possible change of meaning.

8 **Look at the reading text again. Write the verbs in *italics* in the correct columns.**

verb + *to* + infinitive	verb + *-ing*	verb + *to* + infinitive/*-ing*
fail to do something	*avoid doing something*	*remember to do something/ remember doing something*

Get talking

11 Look at the circles. Talk about what is socially acceptable/unacceptable among the people you know in these categories, using some of the verb patterns from this lesson.

Example: *It would be unacceptable in my family if you forgot to send someone a birthday card.*

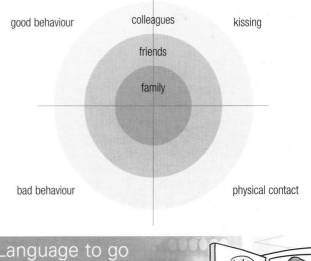

good behaviour — colleagues — kissing
friends
family
bad behaviour — physical contact

Language to go

A: What a surprise! I wasn't expecting to see you.
B: But you knew I was coming to stay! I remember telling you last week.

> GRAMMAR REFERENCE PAGE 110
> PRACTICE PAGE 94

Two cities

Birmingham, Alabama, USA

Speaking and listening

1   Look at the photos of Birmingham (UK) and Birmingham, Alabama (USA). In pairs, talk about the similarities and differences between them.

2   Imagine you had to organise an international conference in one of these cities. What factors would be important? What information would you need to know? In pairs, discuss your ideas.

3   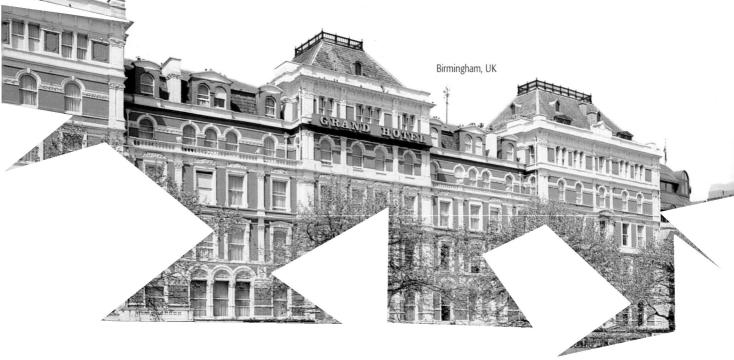 Listen to some information about Birmingham (UK) from a promotional video and decide if the following statements are true or false. Correct the false ones.

Example: Birmingham is in the north of England.
False. Birmingham is in the heart of England.

1   It is difficult to travel to Birmingham.
2   Birmingham is an extremely big city.
3   The Bull Ring is a quiet, old-fashioned English market.
4   The city's orchestra was founded recently.
5   From Birmingham, it is easy to visit the countryside.
6   The speaker thinks Birmingham is a lively city.

4   Listen again. What does the speaker say about the following?

1   Location
2   Characteristics of the city
3   The city's fame

Birmingham, UK

Vocabulary focus

5 **Match these words and expressions from the listening with their definitions.**

1 located in
2 vast
3 in the heart of
4 thriving
5 it is accessible
6 well-established
7 on the outskirts of
8 stunning
9 bustling
10 renowned for
11 charming
12 it is surrounded by
13 cosmopolitan
14 it is within easy reach of
15 vibrant
16 has a worldwide reputation as

Location
a) situated in
b) you can get there easily (*two phrases*)
c) in the centre of
d) on the edge/the outside of
e) around it there is

Characteristics of the city
f) very busy
g) very successful
h) exciting and full of activity
i) with people from all over the world

Describing places (adjectives)
j) extremely beautiful
k) very pleasing/attractive
l) extremely large

The city's fame
m) is famous all over the world as
n) well known and admired for
o) well known for a long time

Practice

6 <u>Underline</u> the correct expressions to complete the text about Birmingham, Alabama.

BIRMINGHAM – ALABAMA, USA

Location ✳

No matter what you are looking for, Birmingham, <u>*in the heart of*</u> / *renowned for* Alabama, has got it all to offer.

History ✳

Founded in 1871, the city of Birmingham soon became a [1] *thriving* / *charming* industrial centre, [2] *on the outskirts of* / *renowned for* its iron and steel production. Birmingham's early growth was so rapid and dramatic that it was nicknamed 'The Magic City'. Whilst historically known for its [3] *bustling* / *well-established* industrial production, a result of [4] *vast* / *accessible* expansion in the late 19th and early 20th centuries, Birmingham's economy now includes both manufacturing and service industries.

Atmosphere ✳

Birmingham, a city of one million inhabitants, has an international flavour and an ethnic diversity that are unusual in the south: it is a genuinely [5] *cosmopolitan* / *vast* city. There's a [6] *renowned* / *vibrant*, exciting environment full of things to do, and it's all right at your front door.

Things to see and do ✳

Visitors to the city can enjoy a wide variety of attractions: stroll through the [7] *cosmopolitan* / *stunning* Botanical Gardens, enjoy eating out in the [8] *charming* / *accessible* restaurants, or visit the [9] *well-established* / *bustling* shopping malls.

Outside attractions ✳

If you like the great outdoors, beautiful mountains, forests and lakes are all [10] *within easy reach of* / *located in the heart of* the city. Or if you're in the mood to explore a little further, you're only a few hours away from Atlanta, New Orleans, the Smoky Mountains and the Gulf beaches.

from website http://main.uab

Get talking ...

7 Choose a city or place you know well and make notes about it under the same headings as in Exercise 6. In groups, talk about your cities to decide on a location for an international conference. Tell the class about the place you chose. Which of the places you heard about would you choose for the conference? Why?

... and writing

8 Write a promotional brochure for the place you chose in Exercise 7.

Language to go

A: It's a thriving, bustling environment in the heart of the city.
B: Mmm ... within easy reach of the motorway, too ...

> PRACTICE PAGE 94

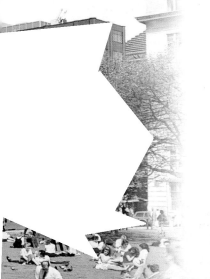

Vocabulary Verb + noun combinations to describe work patterns and habits
Grammar Zero, first and second conditionals
Language to go Talking about consequences

Round the clock

Vocabulary and speaking

1 **Complete the expressions using the words in the box.**

to work *round the clock*
_____

to be _____
_____

to burn _____
_____

the candle at both ends
an early bird
round the clock
a workaholic
the midnight oil
long hours
a night owl
a split shift

2 **In pairs, ask questions using the expressions from Exercise 1, e.g.** *Are you an early bird or a night owl? Why?*

3 **In pairs, discuss whether the following statements are true or false.**

1 Society is moving towards a 24-hour culture.
2 Increasing numbers of people work at night.
3 Longer working hours will mean more absenteeism.
4 Doctors never work 24-hour shifts.
5 Women cope better at working night shifts than men.

Reading

4 **Read the article to see if you were right.**

5 **Answer the following question, then, in pairs, say whether you agree.**

According to the article, what are the advantages and disadvantages of a 24-hour culture?

24 hours a day

IMAGINE THIS: a 24-hour society where nothing ever stops, day or night, a world in which the client never sleeps. In the UK, this is no distant dream. Already there are one million people at work between 9 p.m. and 1 a.m., and if the trend for night working continues, this figure will double in the next ten years.

The possibilities could be endless for the late-night candle-burning types. If you wanted to buy a house, visit a library or an art exhibition, you'd be able to, at any time of the day or night. And that's on top of the telebanking, 24-hour supermarkets and bars, and late-night gyms that we already enjoy.

For employees of the future, the benefits will be enormous. If there are no limits to the beginning and the end of the day, people will be able to spread out their workload, working whenever they choose: day or night. That will mean less stress. And if people were less stressed, there would be less absenteeism.

There will be dangers, however, for this new breed of daytime sleepers. Night work can affect mood, self-esteem and optimism. Problem-solving skills are also diminished, so if you have an important decision to make, it is more difficult. This is worrying, when you consider that thousands of junior doctors already work 24-hour shifts.

Interestingly, research shows that women may be better at coping with shift work than men; those who have had babies are better at dealing with broken sleep patterns. So, if you are not only a night owl, but also female, you are likely to have a better chance of adapting to the round-the-clock life of the future.

from *The Independent* newspaper

Grammar focus

6 **Complete these rules about conditional sentences, then say which conditional is used to describe the following situations.**

- *If* + _____ + _____ (zero conditional)
  If you have an important decision to make, it is more difficult.
- *If* + _____ + _____ (first conditional)
  If the trend continues, this figure will double in the next ten years.
- *If* + _____ + _____ (second conditional)
  If you wanted to buy a house, […] you'd be able to.

1 a probable situation in the future (real)
2 a less likely or hypothetical situation (unreal)
3 a habit or general truth (real)

7 **Answer these questions.**

1 Which of these sentences is the most formal?

As long as
Provided that | *you enjoy working at night, this is a good development.*

2 Can *provided that* and *as long as* be replaced by *if*?
3 Do these two sentences mean the same?

Decisions are more difficult | *if you don't get*
unless you get | *enough sleep.*

Practice

8 **Look at the following situations and decide how likely they are for you and the others in your class (certain/likely/very unlikely). Which type of conditional would be most appropriate for each one?**

1 You oversleep on your first day at work.
2 Your boss expects you to work late into the night on a regular basis.
3 Your partner wants to go to an all-night party, but you have to get up early in the morning.
4 It is nearly the end of the day, and you still haven't finished all your work.
5 You can't get to sleep and you have an important meeting in the morning.
6 A 24-hour supermarket is going to open near your house.
7 You have got an important exam, so you study until late at night.
8 Your baby daughter keeps you awake at night.
9 You are going to work a 24-hour shift.
10 You work out in the gym late at night after a long day's work.

9 **Choose some of the above situations and write questions, using different tenses.**

Example: *What would you do if you overslept on your first day at work?*

Get talking

10 **In groups, ask other students the questions you prepared in Exercise 9. Who in your group is 'an early bird' and who is 'a night owl'? Tell the class.**

Language to go

A: If there's work to be done, he works round the clock.
B: If I had to do that, I'd be exhausted.

> GRAMMAR REFERENCE PAGE 111
> PRACTICE PAGE 95

Vocabulary Adjectives for describing people's characters
Function Describing personality
Language to go Talking about people you know

Person to person

Vocabulary and speaking

1 **Look at the adjectives in the box, which are used for describing people. Match them with the definitions.**

> moody sensitive easy-going cheerful self-confident
> thoughtful dull opinionated big-headed pushy

Example: boring or uninteresting *dull*

1 with a happy character
2 with a relaxed manner or attitude
3 believing in your own abilities or character
4 having a frequently changing state of emotions or attitude and often feeling angry
5 holding strong views and refusing to listen to other opinions
6 easily hurt, very aware of others' feelings and moods
7 thinking about treating other people with care
8 always trying to get what you want (aggressively)
9 believing, and telling everyone, that you are the best

2 **In pairs, discuss which of the adjectives in Exercise 1 you could use to describe yourself, a colleague or a member of your family.**

Example: *I'm sometimes moody, especially in the mornings because I don't like getting up early and going to work.*

Listening

3  **Listen to the extract from a TV programme and answer the questions.**

1 What's the difference between a blind date and a normal date?
2 Have you ever seen a programme like this?
3 Look at the photos of Lara and Dean. What can you guess about their personalities? Try to use some of the vocabulary from Exercise 1.

4 🔊 **Listen to Lara and Dean giving their impressions of each other after their date and answer the questions.**

1 Where did they go on their blind date?
2 What does Lara think of Dean?
3 What does Dean think of Lara?

5 **Look at these sentences. What exactly did they say? Listen again to check.**

Example: Lara **comes across** as quite shy at first …

1 … but once you _____ her, she's got a wicked sense of humour.
2 She's the _____ you can have a good time with.
3 The thing that _____ you _____ Dean is that he's so self-confident.
4 He can be _____ opinionated.
5 There's _____ quite pushy _____ him.
6 The thing I _____ is that he's always _____ you laugh.
7 He's a _____ idiot.

Language focus

6 🔊 **Put the headings with the correct groups of expressions. Then listen and mark the stresses on the phrases.**

1 Describing the type of things a person does.
2 Describing how you feel about someone.
3 First impressions.
4 Describing what the person is like.

a • She comes across as …
  • The thing that strikes you about him is …

b • Once you get to know her …
  • The thing I like about him is that …
  • He makes me (happy/feel good).

c • She's the sort of person who …
  • He's always -ing.

d • There's something … about him.
  • She's a bit (+ *adjective*).
  • He's a bit of a (+ *noun/adjective and noun*).

Practice

7 **Rewrite the following sentences, using the words in brackets.**

Example: At first Mark seems very intense, but actually he isn't. (across)
At first Mark comes across as very intense, but actually he isn't.

1 She tells really funny jokes all the time. (makes)
2 I like Jane because she believes in herself and she isn't shy about expressing her views. (thing)
3 She's always talking about herself. (something)
4 The first thing you notice about him is how relaxed and calm he is. (strike)
5 He's very opinionated. (sort)
6 She never stops gossiping. (always)
7 One minute he's happy, the next he's sad. (bit)

Get talking …

8 **Think of six famous people and imagine what their characters are like. In pairs, describe them. Which couples might be suitable for a blind date? Why?**

… and writing

9 **Write a short text (120–180 words) about a couple you know well.**

Language to go

A: What's your new flatmate like?
B: Once you get to know him, he's very sensitive.

> GRAMMAR REFERENCE PAGE 111
> PRACTICE PAGE 95

35

Vocabulary   Weather idioms used for personality
Grammar   Expressions of probability
Language to go   Talking about how likely things are to happen

Positive thinking

Vocabulary and speaking

1 **Look at these examples of weather and temperature used to describe character.**

	is rather **dull**.	
	is a **cold** / **warm**	person.
He/She	is very **chilled out**.	
	makes heavy weather of something.	
	can be **hot-tempered**.	
	is always **bright and breezy**.	

How would you describe someone who ...

Example: is always very relaxed about life?
very chilled out

1 gets angry very easily?
2 is very friendly?
3 is very unfriendly?
4 generally smiles and has a positive attitude?
5 is a bit boring?
6 tends to overcomplicate things?

2 **Look at the pictures in the text. How would you describe these characters?**

Reading and speaking

3 **Do the questionnaire and discuss your answers in pairs.**

4 **Look at the key on page 85. Is the statement about you true? Tell your partner.**

OPTIMIST OR PESSIMIST?

1 How do you see your future?

a *You'll probably* live to the age of 90, full of energy. *You certainly won't* be sitting around at home!

b *You are quite likely to* get run over by a bus any day, so it's not really worth thinking about.

c You are looking forward to retiring and enjoying an easy life. *You are sure to* have a few problems but nothing serious.

2 Someone you have met at work has invited you to a party. How do you feel?

a Very excited. *You are sure to* meet lots of new and interesting people and have a great evening.

b *You'll probably* stay at home because you certainly won't know anyone there and *it is likely to* be deadly boring.

c *You are fairly convinced that you will* enjoy it. Your new colleague seems friendly enough and *it's inevitable that you'll* meet at least a few new faces.

3 You have arranged to go for a picnic with friends.

a *It's bound to* be a beautiful, sunny day – the hottest this year.

b *You expect it will* rain. It always does when you plan something nice.

c *It's quite possible that it will* be warm and *there's a fair chance that you'll* catch at least a little sunshine.

4 You have just completed a psychological test about how positive thinking can influence the rest of your life.

a *It's unlikely that* anything negative *will* ever happen to you again. It's all in the mind!

b What rubbish! How can you think positively when so many terrible things *are certain to* happen to you?

c *You are not convinced that it will* change your life but *you'll probably* try and adopt a positive outlook and see how long it lasts.

Grammar focus

5 Look at these examples of expressions of future probability from the questionnaire. They fit the patterns in the table. Complete the table with the other expressions in *italics* in the text.

- *It's bound to* be a beautiful, sunny day.
- *It's quite possible that* it will be warm.
- *You are fairly convinced that* you will enjoy it.
- *You will probably stay* at home.

is/are + phrase + *to* ... It's bound to ...	is + adjective + *that* ... *will* It's quite possible that it will ...
phrase (+ *that*) ... *will* You are fairly convinced that you will ...	*will* + adverb/adverb + *won't* You'll probably ...

6 Write these expressions in the correct section of the above table.

I'd imagine that ...   ... definitely won't
... probably won't   It's doubtful that ...
It's likely that ...

Practice

7 Rewrite the phrases in *italics* using the words in brackets, so that the meaning stays the same. Be careful – you may have to change the word order.

Example: You'll certainly receive a reply soon. (sure)
You're sure to receive a reply soon.

1 *There's a fair chance that* I'll change my job before the end of the year. (possible)
2 In the next ten years, average temperatures *will probably* go up slightly and there *is bound to be* a lot more rain. (likely; certain)
3 *I'd imagine that* life will be better for my children than it was for me, as they'll have all sorts of opportunities I never had. (convinced)
4 *It's unlikely that* computers will change our way of life much in the next few years. (doubtful)
5 *It's inevitable that* advances in science and medicine will affect our lives. *I'd imagine that* I'll be able to live until I am over 100 years old. (certainly; possible)
6 This weekend it *will certainly* be sunny. (bound)

8 a) ▭▭ Listen to check your answers to Exercise 7.

b) Listen again, marking the stress on the emphasised words. Repeat the sentences, concentrating on your stress and intonation.

Example: You're sure to receive a reply soon.

Get talking

9 In groups, discuss the predictions in Exercise 7. Do you agree with them? As a group, are you optimistic or pessimistic?

Language to go

A: There's a fair chance it will be sunny later.
B: Yes, but if I don't take my umbrella with me, it's bound to rain.

> GRAMMAR REFERENCE PAGE 111
> PRACTICE PAGE 96

LESSON 18
Vocabulary

Vocabulary 1   Expressions with *money*
Vocabulary 2   Financial terms
Language to go   Talking about money

Money talks

Vocabulary and speaking

1   **Discuss which of these 'money' expressions you would use to describe the pictures. Do you know any others? Think of an example sentence for each expression.**

MONEY

1 to run out of _____
2 to earn good _____
3 it's worth a lot of _____
4 to raise _____
5 it's a waste of _____
6 pocket _____
7 it's good value for _____

Listening

2   🔲 **Listen to Bruce Armstrong, a British writer, and Vladimir Antonyuk, a Russian businessman, talking about money. Then answer the following question.**

How has their financial situation changed and why?

3   **Read the following sentences about Bruce and Vlad. Listen again and <u>underline</u> the correct information. What did they say on the recording that helped you to answer?**

Example: Bruce *has never had much money* / *used to be a millionaire*.

1 Bruce *never had any work* / *did a variety of jobs*.
2 Bruce used to *owe the bank money* / *save a little money*.
3 Now Bruce *is looking for a house to buy* / *lives well but works*.
4 Vlad says that the financial situation changed because *foreigners got involved in the Russian market* / *businesses improved their methods*.
5 Vlad thinks capitalism meant *most people earned more money* / *a few businesspeople started to get rich*.
6 Vlad says older people in Russia still live off the money that *the government gives them* / *they earned from capitalism*.

Vocabulary focus

4 Match the phrases from the listening with the correct definitions. Use the recording script on page 119 if necessary.

inherit money   (be) well-off
(be) overdrawn   (be) hard up
(be able to) afford something
(receive/get) a pension   invest
(have some) savings
(pay) the bills   (take out) a loan
(receive) an income
(pay off) a mortgage   make a profit
(earn/get) (a) bonus(es)
(earn/receive) (a) wage(s)

Money received ...
1 when someone dies and leaves you money in their will (*verb*)
2 when you retire from work
3 when you borrow from the bank
4 in addition to your salary (often for good work)
5 every week (for work by the hour)
6 when a business earns more than it spends (*verb*)
7 regularly (from any source)

Financial state
8 be quite rich
9 be poor
10 owe money to the bank
11 have enough money for something in particular
12 have money invested (in a bank)

Money spent ...
13 to pay for your house
14 to pay for gas, water, telephone etc.
15 usually on a business, hoping to gain more money (*verb*)

5 ▭ Put the words into the correct column according to their pronunciation of the letter 'o', then listen to check.

m<u>o</u>ney   well-<u>o</u>ff   pr<u>o</u>fit   l<u>oa</u>n
b<u>o</u>nus   inc<u>o</u>me   <u>o</u>verdrawn

sh<u>o</u>t	sh<u>ow</u>	sh<u>u</u>t
profit		

Practice

6 Complete the texts with a suitable word or phrase from Exercise 4.

1 Student life
University students often complain of being <u>hard up</u>. In England, they can take out a _____ from the bank, but many of them are still _____ . They can't _____ to go out to expensive restaurants, but drink in cheap student bars instead. Often they need to get part-time jobs in order to _____ the _____ . When their student days are over, many are relieved to find that they can finally get a job and start to receive an _____ to help them pay off their debts.

2 Entrepreneurs
Some entrepreneurs start their businesses from their own home. If they want to expand, they need to persuade people to give them money to _____ in their company. At first, most small companies do not _____ a _____ . However, if you have great reserves of energy and enthusiasm and a bit of luck, you'll be able to employ lots of people to do all the hard work for you. Then, when you are really _____ , you can lie by the pool and award yourself a huge _____ every year.

Get talking

7 In groups, answer the questionnaire.

Money, money, money ...

- What things do you enjoy spending money on? What do you think is a waste of money?
- How do students in your country finance their studies?
- Do you give money to beggars on the street? What about musicians?
- Have you ever found money on the street? How much?
- Do you think it's right that people receive a pension in their old age?
- What do you think is the easiest way to save money?
- What is the quickest way to make money honestly?

Language to go

A: Would you lend me five pounds, Jim? I'm really hard up
B: You mean you can't afford another beer! Here you are.

> PRACTICE PAGE 96

19
The past

Vocabulary Disaster verbs and prepositions
Grammar Future in the past
Language to go Talking about things you were going to do

Unlucky for some

Vocabulary and speaking

1 **Match the phrasal verbs with their meanings.**

1 burn (something) down
2 write (something) off
3 break down
4 trip up
5 knock (something) over
6 fill (something) up
7 cheer (someone) up
8 knock (someone) out

a) develop a problem and stop working
b) destroy by fire
c) knock your foot against something and fall down
d) hit something so that it falls
e) damage something (usually a car) so badly that it isn't worth repairing
f) hit someone so they lose consciousness
g) make a sad person feel happier
h) add something until there is no more space

2 **Think of what might go wrong in each of the following situations. Discuss in pairs, using the phrasal verbs in Exercise 1 and the picture in the text.**

1 you try to save an animal in distress
2 two people get married
3 you pour yourself a drink
4 someone buys an old moped

Reading

3 **Read what actually happened in these situations to see if you were correct.**

1 Mary Kent's car broke down in Richmond Park. Then a duck landed on her head while it was flying and knocked itself out. She was going to rescue the poor bird when a policeman arrived on a motorbike and arrested her for trying to steal the duck.

2 Keith Granby and Cathy Taylor were due to get married in St George's Church when vandals set fire to the church. They refused to give up their plans and went to the reception hall for the party afterwards. Unfortunately, soon after the party started, there was another fire and the hall burnt down.

3 DJ Ian Dockary lost £10,000 worth of karaoke equipment, wrote off his Mazda car in an accident, and caused £3,000 worth of damage to a hired Escort car. He was about to have a good, strong drink to cheer himself up when he fell over, knocked over the drinks cabinet and destroyed £1,000 worth of spirits.

4 Gillie Lambert, from London, had a particularly unlucky week with her moped. Within the space of five days, it was stolen twice and crashed three times. After retrieving it, she was on the point of filling it up with petrol to take it safely home, when the moped burst into flames at the petrol station.

Grammar focus

4 Look at these sentences from the texts, then choose the correct answer.

She *was going to rescue* the poor bird.
He *was about to have* a good, strong drink.
She *was on the point of filling* it *up*.
[They] *were due to get* married.

1 *was/were going to (do something)* is used to talk about:
   a) continuous actions in the past
   b) things we intended to do in the past, but which we didn't do

2 *was/were about to (do something)* is used to talk about:
   a) things we intended to do very soon, but didn't do
   b) things we enjoyed regularly

3 *was/were on the point of (doing something)* is used to talk about:
   a) things we intended to do very soon, but didn't do
   b) things we intended to do much later

4 *was/were due to (do something)* is used to talk about:
   a) an arranged event
   b) an unplanned event

Practice

5 Look at the pictures. In pairs, invent a background to each situation and write what was going to happen.

Example:

He is a footballer and maybe he was going to play for his country, but then he was injured.

Get talking ...

6 In pairs, read your story and plan how you will retell it to your partner. Can you use the 'future in the past'? Then listen to your partner's story and make notes.

Student A: Turn to page 84.   Student B: Turn to page 86.

... and writing

7 Use the notes you made in Exercise 6 to rewrite your partner's story.

Language to go

A: I was about to call you!
B: Really? I was hoping you were going to rescue me!

from *ES Magazine*

> GRAMMAR REFERENCE PAGE 112
> PRACTICE PAGE 97

Vocabulary   Adverbs of intensity
Grammar   *So/such*
Language to go   Talking about journeys

Taxi!

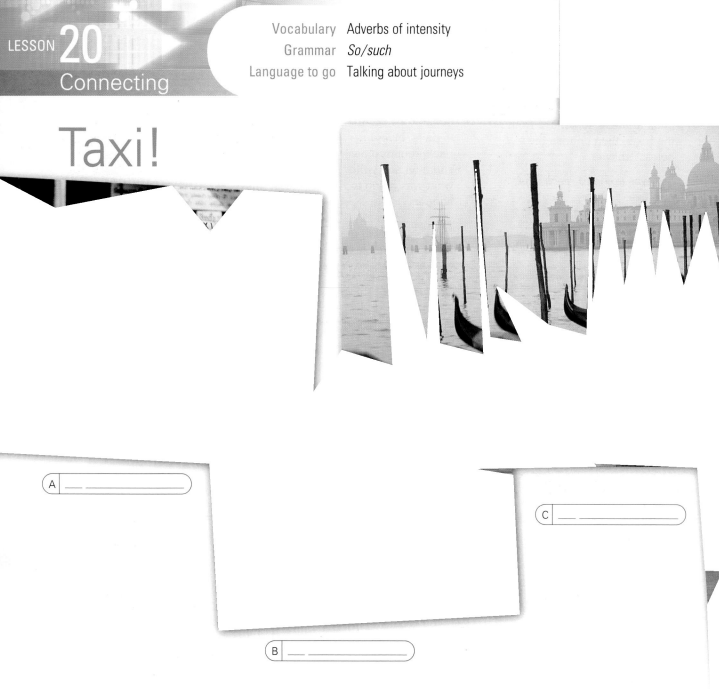

A| __ _____

C| __ _____

B| __ _____

Speaking and listening

1   **In groups, discuss the following questions.**

1   What is the public transport like in your town/city?
2   Have you used public transport in another city/country? How does it compare?
3   Are taxis expensive/easy to find?

2   **Look at the photos and answer the questions.**

1   In which country or city are these types of taxi found?
2   What do you think a taxi ride in them would be like (cost, comfort, speed and general enjoyment)?

3   🔘 **Listen to five people speaking about taking a taxi in different countries. Number the photos in order, and write the name of the country in the gap. Did the speakers share your opinions?**

Vocabulary

4   **a) Look at these sentences from the listening. Which intensifier (in *italics*) makes the adjective stronger, and which makes it weaker?**

You are in the middle of this *totally* fascinating chaos.
The rickshaws you take in India are *quite* light.

b) Put the words from the box in the correct columns.

| very   rather   really   particularly   fairly   pretty |
| totally   quite   absolutely   a little bit   slightly |

weak	strong
rather	very

D 2 London, England

E _____

Grammar focus

5 a) Complete the sentences with *so* or *such,* used to express emphasis, then look at the recording script on page 119 to find other examples.

1 It's _____ hot that you practically stick to the plastic seats.
2 They have _____ interesting stories ... that you don't want to get out.

b) Complete the rules with *so* or *such.*

_____ (+ adjective) + noun

_____ + adjective

Practice

6 Complete the dialogues, using an intensifier + adjective, or *so/such*. Use the words in the box. Several answers may be possible.

> wonderful amazing good imaginative excellent awful
> terrible interesting sunny relaxing enjoyable boring
> ugly

Example: A: How was your holiday?
B: It was **absolutely awful**. It rained every day and I was sick.

1 A: Did you enjoy the last film you saw at the cinema?
  B: Yes. It was _____ that I went to see it again the following day.
2 A: Do you like modern art?
  B: Not that much. I find a lot of it _____ .
3 A: Did you have a nice weekend?
  B: Yes, thanks. It was _____ . I lay in my hammock for two days!
4 A: How was that book you were reading the other day?
  B: It was _____ a/an _____ story that I finished it in one day!
5 A: Do you like doing housework?
  B: Not really. I find most of it _____ .
6 A: Do you watch much television?
  B: Yes. I find the nature programmes _____ .
7 A: Do you listen to classical music?
  B: A little, but I find most of it _____ that it usually sends me to sleep.

7 📟 Listen to the recording to hear some possible answers to Exercise 6. How do the speakers use intonation to show enthusiasm? Practise the sentences.

8 In pairs, ask each other some of the questions from Exercise 6. Reply using intensifiers or *so/such*.

Get talking

9 Make notes about a memorable journey (it could be by taxi or any other means of transport). Think about the following.

- Starting point and destination
- What made it memorable?
- Speed, comfort and cost
- General enjoyment
- Other people involved

In groups, describe your memorable journeys.

Language to go

A: How was your journey?
B: Rather boring and very uncomfortable! And it was such a long way!

> GRAMMAR REFERENCE PAGE 112
> PRACTICE PAGE 97

Vocabulary News, events and disasters
Grammar Passives
Language to go Describing important events

(A)

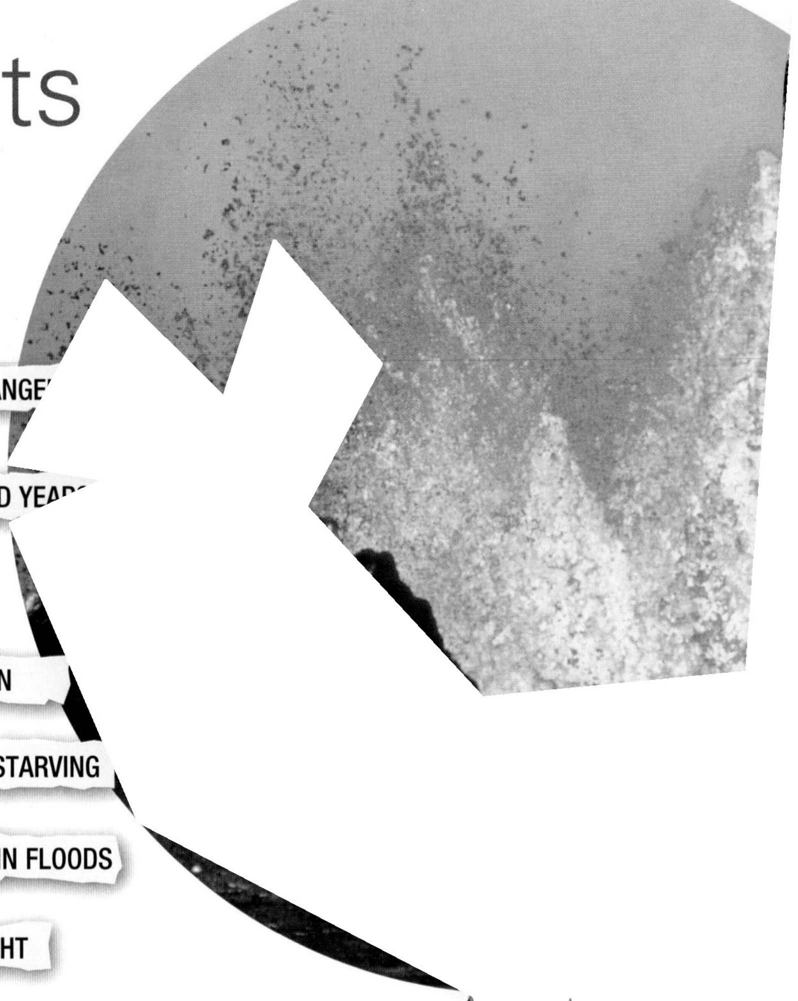

Major events

Vocabulary

1 **Choose one of the following newspaper headlines for each photo.**

1 EARTHQUAKE DEVASTATES LOS ANGE'

2 VOLCANO ERUPTS AFTER FOUR HUNDRED YEA''

3 CIVIL WAR BREAKS OUT

4 BOMB GOES OFF ON TRAIN

5 FAMINE RESULTS IN THOUSANDS STARVING

6 WOMAN RESCUED FROM DROWNING IN FLOODS

7 SUDAN SUFFERS DROUGHT

8 SCIENTISTS MAKE CANCER BREAKTHROUGH

2 **Find verbs in the headlines which mean the following.**

Example: starts/happens suddenly
erupts

1 destroys/does great damage
2 starts
3 dying of hunger
4 dying because they were underwater and couldn't breathe
5 explodes (is activated)

3 **Find nouns which mean the following.**

1 there is no rain so food cannot grow
2 a lot of water covering a normally dry area
3 important development/achievement
4 war between people of the same country
5 extreme lack of food (because the country can't grow any)

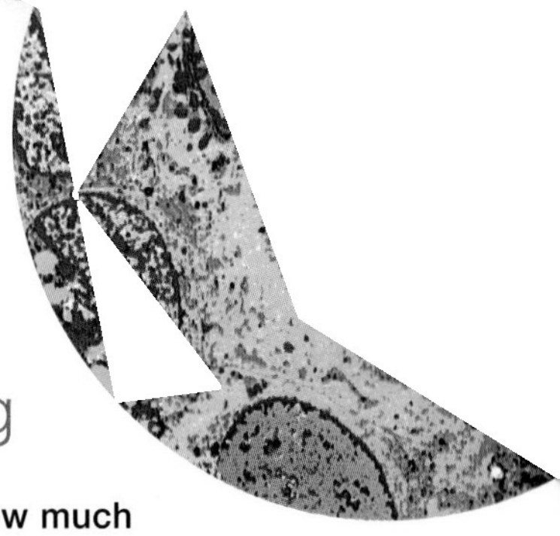

Speaking and listening

4 **In pairs, do this quiz to find out how much you know about important 20th-century events.**

(D)

1 When did man first walk on the moon?
a) the fifties b) the sixties c) the seventies
2 When did the Berlin Wall go up and come down?
a) 1961/1998 b) 1961/1989 c) 1945/1980
3 When did the South African system of apartheid start and finish?
a) 1900/1980 b) 1950/2000 c) 1948/1991
4 When was AIDS first recognised worldwide as a major disease?
a) the nineties b) the eighties c) the seventies
5 When did computer viruses become a big problem?
a) the seventies b) the eighties c) the nineties

5 **[CD] Listen to part of a TV programme and check your answers to Exercise 4.**

(B)

(C)

Practice

8 **In pairs, say if the following sentences are active or passive. Which form is more appropriate for each? Why? Change the sentence if necessary.**

Example: In 1968 someone murdered black civil rights leader, Martin Luther King.
active, but passive is more appropriate (rules 1 and 2)
In 1968 black civil rights leader, Martin Luther King, was murdered.

1 In the end, the brave, handsome, Chicago-based multimillionaire, John Tomes, rescued the economy.
2 One of the greatest technological developments occurred when Alexander Graham Bell invented the telephone in 1876.
3 People hope that a doctor will find a cure for cancer in the future.
4 The world high-jump record, which has stood for over twenty years, was broken this afternoon by the remarkable Leslie Mbeki.
5 If people don't reduce pollution on a world scale, there will be terrible consequences for the environment.
6 They made the shoes, which she wore at the Milan fashion show, in France.
7 A terrible train crash has killed 60 people in southern India.

9 📖 **Listen to check your answers to Exercise 8. What do you notice about the pronunciation of the auxiliary verbs *was*, *were* and *have been*? Repeat the sentences, focusing on the correct pronunciation.**

Get talking

10 **In groups, prepare to talk about major events in a country of your choice. Choose a period of time (it could be a decade, a few years or just one year) which has been of significance to the country. Think about some of the following:**

- wars
- political change
- economic change
- natural events or disasters
- fashions
- youth movements
- great occasions

Make some notes. Explain to the rest of the class why you chose this particular time.

Grammar focus

6 **Look at the following sentences and answer the questions.**

A The Berlin Wall *was built* in 1961.
B Some men *built* the Berlin Wall in 1961.

1 Which sentence is passive?
2 Which sentence is more appropriate? Why?

7 **Look at the recording script on page 119 and find at least one example of the passive for each of these rules.**

With the passive (*be* + past participle), ...

1 we can omit the person who does the action, if they are unknown or unimportant;
2 we often put new information at the end of the clause, to emphasise it;
3 we use *by* to say who/what is responsible for an action.

Language to go

A: All our problems were caused by the last government.
B: That's what we were told by the last government!

> GRAMMAR REFERENCE PAGE 112
> PRACTICE PAGE 98

LESSON 22
Vocabulary

Vocabulary 1 Street personalities
Vocabulary 2 Phrases with *get* and *take*
Language to go Talking about city life

Street life

Speaking and vocabulary

1 **Discuss the following in pairs.**

1 Do you enjoy walking around your home town/city?
2 What don't you like about the town/city? Is there anywhere you wouldn't go?

2 **Match the people you might find in the street with the activities they might do.**

1 busker
2 fortune teller
3 street vendor
4 pedestrian
5 homeless person

a) read your palm
b) ask for change
c) walk in the streets
d) sell you something
e) make music

Reading

3 **a) Read the introduction to an article about street life in Tokyo and London and look at the photos. What similarities and differences do you think they will mention?**

Kate Hayward is an Englishwoman living in Tokyo. Mikako Shimika comes from Japan but now lives in London. They describe the street life in their adopted cities.

b) In pairs, read the two texts about London and Tokyo to check your answers.

Student A: Turn to page 84.   Student B: Turn to page 86.

4 **a) Read your text again and make brief notes in the table.**

city	travelling around	professional entertainers	the homeless	street fashion
Tokyo				
London				

b) Tell your partner about your text and complete the table for the other city. Which city would you prefer to spend time in? Why? Tell your partner.

Vocabulary focus

5 **Find phrases in the texts which mean the same as the definitions below.**

get

Example: get _around_   move from place to place

1 get _____ travel to (a place)
2 get _____ become familiar with
3 get _____ have (something done)
4 get _____ find (something/someone)
5 get _____ become busy (with lots of people)

take

6 take _____ use (a mode of transport)
7 take _____ you expect something and aren't surprised by it
8 take _____ happen
9 take _____ use an opportunity for your own benefit
10 take _____ give you a shock because you were not expecting something
11 take _____ not be in a hurry
12 take no _____ pay no attention to

Practice

6 **Complete the sentences with phrases from Exercise 5.**

Example: I hate travelling on the Underground in rush hour – it _gets so crowded_.

1 People don't always appreciate their city; they've lived there for so long that they _____ .
2 I think you need at least a month to _____ a city, especially all the little areas and streets.
3 In cities, everyone is always rushing, but in the countryside people tend to _____ .
4 It's easy to _____ in Zurich. There are buses, trams and trains and they're all simple to use.
5 You should _____ being in Paris. You've always wanted to practise your French!
6 I thought the weather in London would be terrible, but it was so sunny that it _____ and I had to buy some sunglasses.

Get talking ...

7 **In groups, imagine you are members of a tourist authority. Your task is to create more street life so that:**

- more tourists will come
- people will have more to see and do on the streets
- it will be easier to travel around the city

Discuss how you will achieve these aims using the ideas in the picture. Report to the rest of the class.

... and writing

8 **Write a proposal, explaining how you will achieve the aims in Exercise 7.**

Language to go

A: How do you get around your city?
B: I normally take the bus.

> PRACTICE PAGE 98

Vocabulary   Crimes and criminals
Grammar   Third and mixed conditionals
Language to go   Describing how things could have been different

Gun crazy

Speaking and vocabulary

1 **In groups, discuss the following issues.**

1 Do you think that changing gun laws could influence the amount of violent crime on the streets? Why/Why not? What do you think could change this?
2 Do you think that police should carry guns?
3 Would you ever consider keeping a gun for self-defence?

2 **Explain the difference between the following criminals.**

1 a mugger and a burglar
2 a smuggler and a hijacker
3 a hitman and a murderer
4 a shoplifter and a pickpocket
5 a terrorist and a kidnapper

3 **Say which of the criminals in Exercise 2 does the following.**

1 is involved in violent crime
2 steals possessions or money
3 kills people for money
4 may have political motives
5 steals from houses

Speaking and reading

4 **Look at the photo of Ellen Stutzenbaker in the article, where she describes how she nearly shot someone, then answer the questions.**

1 Do you think she looks like a violent criminal?
2 Why do you think she nearly shot someone?

5 **Read the article and answer the questions.**

1 When did Ellen get involved with guns?
2 Why did she nearly shoot the lady?
3 How does she feel about what happened?
4 What does she think about the Arkansas shootings?

6 **Decide whether you agree with Ellen's views.**

'I'm sure I would have shot her'

A **frightening** rise in violent crime and 'accidental' shootings has left Americans asking themselves if they should continue to teach their children to shoot. Ellen Stutzenbaker, 24, thinks that they should, despite nearly having shot an old lady 'by mistake'.

'I was living with an older lady and she was supposed to be away. I thought I was in the house alone and I heard a noise from downstairs. Then I heard someone outside my door so I started to load my automatic. As I was reaching for some shells, though, I dropped them on the floor. Luckily, she heard me drop the shells and said "hello". It was only then that I realised who it was. If she'd walked through the door I think I would have shot her. Actually, I'm sure I would have shot her because you don't wait around to see who it is – you just shoot, and that's it. It makes me feel good because you never really know what you're going to do in that situation, and I was ready.'

Ellen started shooting when she was only twelve. She always keeps a rifle in her room and she hunts regularly.

'I heard about one of the kids in Arkansas who shot his classmates at school. His grandfather had taught him how to use a gun, and I think it was a good idea. Some say that if he hadn't been taught to shoot, perhaps the whole thing would never have happened. But that's not really the case; the shootings didn't happen because he was able to shoot. He had psychological problems; it was his mental state.'

from *The Week* magazine

Grammar focus

7 **Look at these sentences and answer the questions.**

if + past perfect   + past conditional
If she**'d walked** through the door, I **would have shot** her.

   past conditional   + *if* + past perfect
I **would have shot** her *if* she**'d walked** through the door.

1 Did Ellen shoot the lady?
2 Why/Why not?
3 How does the meaning change in this sentence?
   If she'd walked through the door,
   I might have/could have shot her.

8 **Look at this sentence and <u>underline</u> the correct answers below.**

If + past perfect   + present conditional
If she'd fired the gun, I probably *wouldn't be* here today.

1 The first clause refers to the *present / past*.
2 The second clause refers to the *present / past*.
3 This is a *third / mixed conditional*.

Practice

9 **Put the verbs in brackets into a suitable tense.**

Example: They installed a new alarm system. If they **hadn't put** (put) it in, they **would have been** (be) burgled.

1 The police were armed. If they _____ (have) guns, the thieves _____ (shoot) them.
2 The terrorists were released from prison. If the politicians _____ (change) the laws, the prisoners _____ still _____ (be) inside.
3 The police had been informed about the robbery. If they _____ (know), they _____ (catch) the thieves.
4 Someone stole my wallet. If the bus _____ (be) so crowded, I _____ (notice) what was happening.
5 She didn't pay for her shopping. If she _____ (be) such an old lady, she _____ (be) arrested.
6 The owner of the house shot the young man. If he _____ (try) to burgle the house, he _____ (be) alive today.

Get talking

10 **In pairs, discuss how you think the following situations could have been different.**

- Thieves planning to steal diamonds worth £350 million from the Millennium Dome in London were caught by police who had been warned of the plan. The police were waiting, dressed as cleaners, with guns in black plastic bags.
- A 40-year-old farmer was sent to prison in the UK for shooting a young burglar who entered his home.
- An elderly English couple, living off a small pension, regularly went to France. They smuggled cheap wine and cigarettes into the UK and sold them for a profit. Eventually they were arrested.

Language to go

A: If we'd planned it better, we wouldn't have been caught.
B: If you hadn't forgotten the gun, we might have escaped!

> GRAMMAR REFERENCE PAGE 112
> PRACTICE PAGE 99

Difficult situations

Vocabulary and speaking

1   **Look at the picture and make sentences about it using the vocabulary below. What is wrong in each case and what should be done?**

Example: **The food is off. It needs throwing away.**

The	milk/food shirt room TV	is torn. is messy. doesn't work. is off.

It needs/They need	mending. tidying. throwing away. fixing/repairing.

2   **In groups, discuss the following.**

Have you ever ...

1 complained about housework to someone you live with?

2 sent something back because it was of poor quality?

3 complained about poor service?

4 got into trouble at school or at work?

Tell the others when it was and what happened. Would you do any of these things?

Listening

3   📖 **Listen to people in the situations in Exercise 2. Number the situations in the order you hear them. What exactly is the problem in each situation?**

4   **Listen to three of the dialogues again and fill in the gaps.**

1

Waiter: Yes sir, can I help you?

Man: Well, it's **about the** wine. I'm _____ it doesn't taste too good. _____ possibly bring us another one?

Waiter: I'm sorry, sir. I'll _____ what I can _____ .

2

Ann: Neil. Can I have a _____ ?

Neil: Yes. _____ the _____ ?

Ann: I'm afraid I really need to _____ to _____ about your attitude to work.

Neil: What's the problem?

Ann: Well, you just don't seem interested. I've had to warn you about this before, first your appearance, then being late for work, and now this. I'm afraid it _____ good enough.

3

Dave: Marissa. I _____ if I could have a word.

Marissa: What about?

Dave: Well, it's _____ the house.

Marissa: That again? What's the problem now?

Dave: Well, it's a mess. Everything's filthy!

Marissa: What do you want me to do?

Dave: Well, _____ help tidy up a bit more? _____ you _____ do your share of the cleaning? I mean, it _____ be _____ if you washed the dishes now and again ...

focus

boxes below with the correct

. isting
Making suggestions/requests
Introducing the problem
4 Apologising

A ....

- Can I have a word? N
- I don't want to make a fuss, but …
- I'm afraid I need to talk to you about …
- It's about the …

B ....

- It's just not acceptable.
- I'm sorry, but that's just not good enough.
- I really don't see why I should …
- I really must ask you to …

C ....

- Would you mind -ing …?
- Could you possibly …?
- Couldn't you …?
- I wonder/was wondering if you could …?
- It would be nice if you could …

D ....

- I'm really sorry. I didn't realise.
- I'll see what we can do.
- I'm afraid there's nothing I can do.
- I'll do my best.

6 Mark each phrase with an 'F' for formal, an 'I' for informal or an 'N' for neutral. Use the recording script on pages 119–120 to help you.

7 ▭▭ Practise repeating the phrases in Exercise 5. Concentrate on your intonation.

8 In pairs, practise saying the complete dialogues from Exercise 3.

Practice

9 **In pairs, choose two of the following situations and write mini-dialogues using the language from Exercise 5.**

1 Your boss is busy talking to a colleague, but you really need to speak to him.
2 Your bank has still not sent you the statement you requested nearly three months ago.
3 You would like to change a shirt you bought in the shop last week. When you got it home, you noticed there was a small hole in the sleeve.
4 You arrive at the airport to find that the departure time was changed and the flight has already left. You were not informed. You complain to a member of staff.
5 A customer calls you to say that the computer he bought ten years ago is no longer working.
6 You ring the authorities to complain that nobody has been to collect the rubbish for two weeks.

Get talking

10 **In pairs, practise acting out the two dialogues you wrote in Exercise 9. Concentrate on your intonation to convey how you feel about the situation.**

Act out your dialogues to the class.

Language to go

A: Would you mind putting out that cigarette? This is a no-smoking area.
B: I'm really sorry. I didn't realise.

> GRAMMAR REFERENCE PAGE 112
> PRACTICE PAGE 99

Vocabulary   Expressions for annoying habits
Grammar   Present continuous and present simple for de
Language to go   Talking about changing situations

Under pressure

Vocabulary and speaking

1 **Look at the expressions below and answer the questions.**

1 Which are positive and which are negative?
2 Which are neutral and which are informal?

| It | drives me crazy (really) annoys/irritates/bugs me gets on my nerves | if/when/that … |

| I | can't stand it find it stressful like it | when … |

| It's | a relief when/that … comforting to know that … |

2 **In pairs, talk about situations that you find stressful/relaxing (at home/at work/ on the streets/in shops).**

Reading

3 **Read the article and choose the most appropriate title.**

1   **NEW TECHNOLOGY –   FRIEND OR ENE**

2   **HOW LAUGHING CAN IMPROVE YOUR W**

3   **STRESS AND THE IT INDUSTRY**

MOST STRESS today is caused by the very things that are supposed to make life easier, such as mobile phones and pocket organisers.

Stress levels at work, in particular, are on the increase, but Dr John Morreal, of the University of South Florida, suggests humour could be the answer. As well as improving motivation and morale, humour in the workplace can improve a company's productivity by up to 40 per cent.

Humour allows fresh and original ideas to flourish because it removes normal inhibitions and can help improve mental flexibility among workers. 'Modern industries such as computer and IT firms are changing the quickest,' explains Dr Morreal. 'Many now have laughter rooms, full of funny gadgets, where employees can go for some laughter time before a big meeting or a brain-storming session.'

The changes in the United States are catching on among British employers, as they are increasingly aware of the need to create fun environments. Companies are slowly coming to realise the significance of job satisfaction as a key contribution to business performance. And as employees are spending more time at work, humour in the office is becoming more and more important.'

So if you're looking for a stress-free time at work, learn to laugh in the face of your problems.

from *The Independent* newspaper

4 In pairs, decide whether the following statements are true or false.

1 Electronic gadgets, designed to ease stress, actually cause more stress.
2 Dr Morreal suggests that humour may help increase a company's profits.
3 He suggests that laughing after an important meeting is particularly important.
4 Companies in the USA are changing more quickly than those in the UK.

Grammar focus

5 Look at the expressions and answer the questions.

1 Which phrases can be used to talk about numbers?
2 Which can be used to talk about ideas/general trends?

is still going up	is starting to come down
are changing	are catching on
are not following the trend	are slowly coming to realise
are more often -ing	is becoming more and are more (important)
are on the increase	is less and less (more and more) common
are increasingly aware	

6 Look at the graphs and describe them using the different expressions.

Example: *Sales are on the increase.*

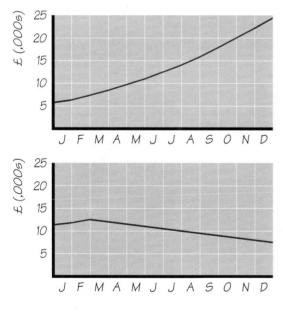

7 Find expressions in Exercise 5 which mean the following.

1 are beginning to understand = _____

2 are behaving differently = _____

Practice

8 Complete the following texts with words or expressions from the box.

> organise   are using   are not catching on
> increasingly popular   are not following the trend
> are taking part   more and more   increase
> continue   starting to come down   are realising

1 In Germany, stressed workers **are using** super-cold (minus 230°F) walk-in freezer therapy to relieve stress. The therapy is becoming _____ among business executives, who use it to condition themselves for important meetings.
2 _____ people _____ that the best way to _____ productivity in a company is to establish a relaxed working atmosphere among the staff. Some bosses, however, _____ and _____ to treat their workers with little or no respect.
3 'In my department, media marketing and sales, we _____ a whole range of "fun" activities for our staff. Amazingly, we have noticed that the number of sick days taken by staff who _____ is _____ . It's a shame that other companies _____ .'

Get talking

9 In groups, choose two or three of the topics below and discuss whether these aspects of our lives are becoming more or less stressful.

> GRAMMAR REFERENCE PAGE 113
> PRACTICE PAGE 100

Language to go

A: Did you know that more and more bosses are using humour at work?
B: Shut up and get on with your work!

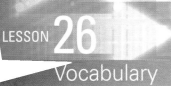

Vocabulary   Phrases to describe houses
Language to go   Talking about homes

At home

Speaking and listening

1   **In pairs, look at the photos of the two houses and answer the questions.**

1   Where do you think these houses are? What kind of people do you think live in them?
2   Do you think the style of someone's house reflects his or her personality?
3   Which house would you choose to live in? Why?

2    **Listen to people talking about the houses in the photos. Write notes about each house in the table.**

House	Where is the house?	Who was it designed for?	Positive features	Negative features
1				
2				

3   **Check your answers. Which house would you prefer to live in now?**

Vocabulary focus

4 **Match the groups of words with the correct categories. Use the recording script on page 120 to help you.**

1 a bedsit/a studio flat/a villa
2 a wooden floor/a rug
3 in the basement/in the loft/on the second floor
4 convenient/isolated/not far from
5 modern/classical/elegant/minimalist
6 spacious/huge/tiny/cramped
7 cosy/intimate
8 high ceilings/tall windows/fireplace
9 chilly/draughty/airy/has central heating
10 overlooks/has a view of
11 brand new/second hand/old-fashioned

a) age
b) type of accommodation
c) floor
d) location
e) style
f) feel/atmosphere
g) size
h) features
i) warm/cold interior
j) view
k) position in the building

Practice

5 **Read Lucy's description of her home. Underline the most suitable word(s) to complete the description.**

The thing I appreciate most about my flat is the balcony. It is _tiny_ / _spacious_ / _airy_, but there is just enough space to sit out in the morning sun and enjoy breakfast. It's covered in flowers and ¹ _overlooks_ / _is overlooked by_ the small garden. The flat is ² _in the basement_ / _on the second floor_ of an old house built in a very ³ _classical_ / _modern_ style with stone floors, tall windows with green shutters and white walls. The furniture is simple. I buy most of it ⁴ _modern_ / _second hand_ / _ancient_ from the local markets – they're ⁵ _a long way from_ / _convenient_ / _not far from_ here – and they have lovely stuff. I don't want too much furniture; the rooms aren't huge and my style is rather ⁶ _modern_ / _classical_ / _minimalist_. In the evenings, I light candles all round the flat and the atmosphere is very ⁷ _huge_ / _spacious_ / _intimate_. On the downside, it can be a bit ⁸ _chilly_ / _airy_ / _cramped_ in the flat as there's no ⁹ _fireplace_ / _central heating_.

6 **In pairs, discuss whether you think the house described would be nice to live in. Why/Why not?**

Get talking

7 **Imagine you are letting out your home (or dream home) for a holiday exchange. Make notes so you can describe it to your group. Think about the following.**

- Where is it located?
- What kind of building is it?
- How big is it?
- In what style is it decorated?
- What furniture does it have in it?
- Positive and negative features? (What do you like/dislike about it?)

In groups, talk about your homes.

Language to go

A: How's your new flat?
B: Fine. It's a bit cramped, but very convenient.

> PRACTICE PAGE 100

N27
The past

Vocabulary US/UK English
Grammar *To be/get used to*
Language to go Describing a personal change of environment

A new beginning

Vocabulary

1 **Say which of these things you can see in the photos.**

1 Tube	5 queue
2 lift	6 petrol station
3 rubbish	7 flat
4 pavement	8 motorway

2 **Match the words from Exercise 1 with their American English equivalents.**

a) gas station	e) subway
b) freeway/expressway	f) sidewalk
c) apartment	g) elevator
d) garbage	h) line

3 **a) Match these American English words with their definitions.**

1 vacation   a) a time between summer and winter
2 fall   b) a list showing how much you have to pay in a restaurant
3 pants   c) a flat, hard cake, sold in packets
4 check   d) a time when you go away for a break
5 cookie   e) food made of sugar, mainly for children
6 candy   f) clothes you wear on your legs

b) Write their British English equivalents.

Listening

4 **a)**  **Listen to Romek Oleksy, who comes from Warsaw but now lives in Chicago. He describes some of the differences between living in the two cities. As you listen, tick (✔) the items in the box which he talks about.**

> differences in vocabulary   size   entertainment
> shopping   attitudes to work   making friends   travel
> traditions   danger in cities   clothes   cost of living

b) In pairs, check your answers. Can you remember any details about what he said? Listen again and check.

Grammar focus

5 Look at the following examples of *used to* from the listening, then match them with how they are used.

1 I *used to take* the tram.
2 I*'m used to* most things.
3 I quickly *got used to* the food.

a) a description of the process of becoming familiar with something
b) a past habit or state that no longer happens now
c) a situation that is familiar or normal, and not strange

6 Choose the correct alternative from the box to complete the three rules.

the infinitive   the *-ing* form or a noun

1 *Used to* is followed by _____ .
2 *Be used to* is followed by _____ .
3 *Get used to* is followed by _____ .

7 Look at these three sentences. What is the rule for *used to* and *use to*?

I *used* to enjoy badminton.
Did you *use* to work here?
I *didn't use* to like football.

Practice

8 Complete the sentences with a form of *used to, be used to* or *get used to*. There may be more than one possible answer.

Example: When I arrived in India, I found it difficult to **get used to** the food.

1 Moving to the village was no problem for me. I had worked in a small town for many years, so I _____ living a quiet life.
2 When my sister heard salsa music for the first time, she wasn't keen on it. She still doesn't love it, but these days, she _____ it.
3 When I changed my job, it was a question of _____ the new working conditions.
4 Don't worry! I know it all seems strange at the moment, but you _____ it.
5 Athletes don't complain about all the training. They _____ it.
6 The majority of people _____ have cars in the old days, because they were so expensive.

Get talking

9 Think about a time when something was new to you. What did you have to get used to? Make notes in the first column.

situation	you	your partner
first day at work		
first day at school		
time in a foreign country		
first time away from home		
someone new in the house		
other?		

Describe the situation to your partner, then listen to him/her and complete the second column.

Language to go

A: I used to be poor and live on the streets, you know.
B: Well, I'm sure you'll get used to your new home.

> GRAMMAR REFERENCE PAGE 113
> PRACTICE PAGE 101

Ⓒ

Animal magic

Speaking and reading

1   **Look at the photos. Can you name these animals?
Which of them do you think can do the following?**

1   follow someone's footprints
2   predict the weather
3   sense a person's fear

Ⓐ

Ⓑ

2   **Read the article about the amazing talents of
animals to find the answers to Exercise 1. When
you have finished, check in pairs.**

3   **In pairs, answer these questions.**

1   How do snakes and sharks detect their prey?
2   How does a ladybird protect itself in winter?

Are human beings **really**
the most advanced
creatures on the planet?

We think we are the most advanced creatures on the
planet. But if we look a little deeper, we will realise that
all our inventions, which make life easier, are really just
copies of things already found in nature. Here are a few
examples of the incredible things animals can do.

We may have invented heat-seeking cameras which
find disaster victims, but snakes can 'see' heat.
Rattlesnakes have sensors which can detect small
changes in temperature. They 'see' us by the heat that
surrounds us, so they can find their prey in the dark.

Even our footprints leave some warmth, which can be
detected long after we have passed. This means snakes
know where we are and where we have been.

We discovered electricity and ways of looking for it.
However, creatures which live in the sea have electro-
sensors which can detect electricity. A swimmer who is
injured gives off electricity – his heartbeat and his
nerves flashing on and off in panic. A shark wouldn't
'see' him through its eyes, which are very small, but it
would feel the swimmer's fear.

We spend millions trying to predict the weather,
using complicated science and equipment. Ladybirds
know, in advance, exactly what kind of winter we will
have. Each autumn, they choose a place to spend the
winter. If it is going to be cold, they find a site where
there is plenty of warmth – for example, under leaves. If
the winter is going to be mild, they go somewhere
where there is more air. Nobody knows how they do it.

Practice

6 Connect the sentences using the appropriate relative pronoun and any necessary punctuation.

Examples: **Non-essential information**
The kingfisher can't swim. It dives into water to catch fish.
The kingfisher, which can't swim, dives into water to catch fish.
Essential information
The penguin is a seabird. It can swim.
The penguin is the seabird which can swim.

Non-essential information
1 The tiger is only found in Asia. It is the largest member of the cat family.
2 Camels are used for trips across the desert. They can drink 113 litres (200 pints) of water in half an hour.
3 The ostrich is the world's tallest bird. It cannot fly.
4 Bee hummingbirds are the smallest bird. They come from the Amazon.
5 Electric eels kill fish by electrocuting them. They eat half of their body weight in food every day.

Essential information
6 The Asian elephant is a large mammal. Its pregnancy lasts 22 months.
7 The anabas is a fish. It can climb trees.
8 The chameleon is a lizard. It can change colour.
9 The mosquito is a malaria-carrying insect. It causes 2,000,000 deaths a year.

7 Listen to check your answers to Exercise 6. Pay attention to how the speaker pauses for non-defining clauses, but not for defining clauses. Say the sentences aloud, pausing where there are commas.

Get talking and writing

8 In groups, write definitions for the words in the crosswords.

Student A: Turn to page 84.   Student B: Turn to page 86.

In pairs, read your clues to each other and try to complete the crossword.

Example: A: What is 2 down?
B: It's a place where there is no water.
A: A desert?
B: Yes!

Grammar focus

4 Look at these sentences from the article, then find the other defining and non-defining relative clauses in the article.

1 A swimmer *who is injured* gives off electricity.

A defining relative clause contains *essential* information about the noun.

2 All our inventions, *which make life easier,* are really just copies …

A non-defining relative clause contains *extra* information about the noun.

5 Complete the rules with *Defining* or *Non-defining.*

_____ clauses are often used in formal writing and are separated by commas at the beginning and the end of the clause.

_____ relative clauses do not have commas.

Language to go

A: Did you know that dolphins, which are mammals, communicate by whistling?
B: No, but I know there's a spider which lives underwater.

> GRAMMAR REFERENCE PAGE 113
> PRACTICE PAGE 101

Verb patterns

Vocabulary   Expressions to describe mood
Grammar   *To have/get something done*
Language to go   Talking about things you have done for you

Treat yourself

Speaking and vocabulary

1 Answer these questions.

  1 What do you do to put yourself in a good mood?
  2 Which of the activities in the photos might you choose?

2 Match the expressions with their meanings.

  1 It cheers me up.
  2 It calms me down.
  3 It makes me feel better.
  4 It takes my mind off any problems.
  5 It helps me get through the day.
  6 It keeps me going.

  a) It makes me think of other things.
  b) It lets me relax if I am feeling anxious or too excited.
  c) It improves my mood (*two expressions*).
  d) It allows me to continue (*two expressions*).

3 Use some of the expressions from Exercise 2 to describe activities which you do.

Example: Listening to music cheers me up.

Reading and speaking

4 Read about what other people do to get into a good mood. Which three people correspond to the photos?

5 In pairs, discuss what keeps *you* going. Do you have similar ideas to the people in the text?

Grammar focus

6 Look at these phrases from the text and answer the questions.

I like to *have everything done* for me.
I *'m getting* my house *redecorated*.
We *have* our newspapers *delivered*.

  1 If you have your newspapers delivered, …
    a) do you do it?
    b) does someone do it for you?

  2 What is the correct structure?
    a) *have/get* + object + infinitive
    b) *have/get* + object + past participle

(A)

Take it easy!

What do you do to put yourself in a good mood?
We asked people all over the world about what cheers them up.

● In Thailand, when you have your hair cut you also get a head massage. This really helps you to relax.
  Wek, Chiang Mai, Thailand

● I like gardening. It keeps me going when I'm feeling stressed. It really helps to take my mind off any problems.
  Werner, Konstanz, Germany

● I'm usually a workaholic, so when I'm on holiday I like to have everything done for me. I go to lots of restaurants, take taxis everywhere, and generally put my feet up.
  Mike, Sydney, Australia

● We have our newspapers delivered on Saturdays, and then we read them in bed. It's the best way to start the weekend.
  Stan, Walsall, UK

Ⓑ

Spending time with my dog puts me in a good mood. I take her for long walks at least three days a week.
Clara, Buenos Aires, Argentina

When I'm feeling fed up, I splash out on new clothes or go looking for bargains in the second-hand market. It always makes me feel better. Either that or I have my nails done.
Tara, Toronto, Canada

I eat chocolate to cheer myself up. I know I shouldn't because it's fattening, but it just helps me get through the day.
Marie, Paris, France

I have quite a big CD collection, and if I need to relax, I listen to classical music. It calms me down and I find I can completely lose myself in the music.
Regina, Recife, Brazil

I'm getting my house redecorated at the moment, so when I'm free, I enjoy doing some of the work myself, especially painting the walls. Actually, I find a lot of DIY quite relaxing.
Thabo, Cape Town, South Africa

Practice

7 **Correct the following sentences.**

Example:
I've lost my keys. I'll have to get a new set ~~to~~ cut tomorrow.
I've lost my keys. I'll have to get a new set cut tomorrow.

1 The car has broken down. I'll have the engine repair tomorrow.
2 I cut my hair yesterday. It was very expensive.
3 I'm having my book to be published next year. The publisher is quite well known.
4 I took my picture by a famous photographer. He made me look beautiful!
5 We need to have fix the heater. I know a good electrician who can do it for us.
6 We redecorated our kitchen last week. But the workers made a terrible mess.

Get talking

8 **Find someone who ...**

- has their hair cut every two months.
- has had their photograph taken in the last week.
- has their eyes tested every two years.
- is going to have something done in their house in the next month.
- would never have food delivered to their house.
- had their teeth checked last month.
- is going to have their car serviced in the next month.

Language to go

A: Don't you think it's time to get your hair cut?
B: But I had it cut last year!

> GRAMMAR REFERENCE PAGE 113
> PRACTICE PAGE 102

LESSON 30
Vocabulary

Vocabulary 1   Ages and stages
Vocabulary 2   Phrasal verbs 2
Language to go   Talking about growing up

Growing up

Vocabulary and speaking

1   **Choose an age range (e.g. *five–ten years old*) for each of the following life stages.**

> toddler   baby   kid   teenager   adolescent
> middle-age   senior citizen   young adult
> thirty-something

2   **Look at the cartoon strip above and identify the stages in the cartoon. In pairs, discuss the questions.**

1   What events in the man's life tell him he's growing up?
2   At what age are people considered to be grown up in your country?
3   How do you know when you are grown up? What does it depend on?

Speaking and listening

3   **Look at the photos. Why do you think these stages in their lives might have been important to these people?**

4   ▭▭ **In pairs, listen to see if you were correct, then discuss.**

5   **In pairs, answer the first question in the table using the ideas in the box.**

> getting up very early   joining the army   smoking a pipe
> making a decision about your career   having children
> being naughty   getting into trouble   listening to stories
> doing what you're told   having a good/bad time at school

Questions	Speaker 1	Speaker 2	Speaker 3
Which ideas do they talk about?			
Which relatives do they talk about?			
How was their relationship?			

6   **Listen again and answer the second and third questions in the table.**

Vocabulary focus

7 Look at the following phrasal verbs from the listening. Who said them?

1 I never thought I would *end up* as a soldier.
2 *Taking on* that sort of responsibility isn't easy.
3 *Making my mind up* about my job wasn't easy.
4 ... when my parents stopped *telling me off* for everything I did
5 (We were) always *picking on* the younger kids.
6 My friends always seemed *to get away with it*.
7 I don't know how she *put up with* me.
8 I always *looked forward to* visiting him.
9 I really *looked up to him* and believed what he said.

8 Check your answers to Exercise 7 with the recording script on page 120 and match the phrasal verbs with their definitions.

a) accept responsibility or work
b) come to be in a situation/state, especially when you didn't plan it
c) admire someone
d) be angry with someone and tell them verbally
e) escape punishment
f) decide
g) choose one person/group of people in particular for something negative
h) wait for something, with excitement
i) endure something difficult (you don't like it but there is nothing you can do)

Practice

9 Complete the texts with the phrasal verbs from Exercise 7 in the correct form.

1 Having a baby meant growing up. No more *getting away with* just having a good time, a carefree existence. Once you've _____ to be a parent, you have this responsibility to set a good example in your life and be someone who your kids can _____ and think 'Yes, that's how I'd like to be when I grow up'. _____ that responsibility was really hard for me. I was still a child myself in many ways.

2 I realised I was an old man when my seventeen-year-old daughter came home late one night with some friends. They started playing music. I'd been _____ getting a good night's sleep, and at about two a.m. I was lying in bed, and the noise was really getting on my nerves. I couldn't _____ it any more and I jumped out of bed and went downstairs. I wanted to _____ them _____ , but then I remembered I had been the same when I was young. I stood at the door and couldn't believe how I had _____ as the boring old parent.

Get talking ...

10 Look at these questions and choose two or three to ask other students. Think of your own answers.

- As a teenager, what kind of things did you look forward to doing when you grew up?
- Did you look up to anyone when you were younger? Who? Why?
- Were you ever told off at school? What kinds of things did you get into trouble for?
- As a child, what did you think you would end up doing when you grew up? Were you right?
- What kinds of things do you find it difficult to put up with? Has this changed with your age?

In groups, discuss the questions. Do you all have similar opinions/experiences?

... and writing

11 Write about two or three important events that happened when you were growing up.

Language to go

A: I never thought I would end up looking after toddlers.
B: No – I don't know how you put up with them!

> PRACTICE PAGE 102

21

Modals

Vocabulary   Word building: measurements
Grammar   Modals for past deduction
Language to go Speculating about life in the past

Monumental mysteries

Vocabulary and speaking

1 Use the words in the table to complete the sentences.

noun	verb	adjective
height	heighten	high
width	widen	wide
weight	weigh	heavy
depth	deepen	deep
length	lengthen	long

Example: Some of the stones at Stonehenge **weigh** over 45 tonnes.

1 The Petronas Towers, Kuala Lumpur, built in 1996, are 452 metres _____ .
2 Lake Baikal, Siberia, has a _____ of 1.63 kilometres (it's the world's deepest lake).
3 The River Nile is 6,670 kilometres _____ (it could stretch all the way from New York to Berlin).
4 The _____est point in the ocean is nearly eleven kilometres down, 25 times the _____ of the Empire State Building.
5 The largest iceberg was approximately 335 kilometres _____ and 100 kilometres _____ , an area three times as big as Cyprus.

2 Look at these photos of famous sights and answer these questions.

1 What do you know about these places?
2 Have you seen any of them?
3 Which are the most beautiful/mysterious?
4 Can you make any guesses about their height/width/ weight?

Reading

3 In groups, read the texts and fill in the appropriate row of the table. Then exchange information to complete the table.

Student A: Turn to page 84.
Student B: Turn to page 86.
Student C: Turn to page 85.

monument	What is it?	Why was it built?	When was it built
Stonehenge			
Easter Island statues			
Machu Picchu			

Machu Picchu

Easter Island

Grammar focus

4 a) In pairs, <u>underline</u> the modal verb phrases which best complete the statements.

1 Stonehenge *might / can't* have been some form of meeting place for tribes.
2 It *must / can't* have taken about 600 people to move each stone.
3 They *could / can't* have floated the stones across the river.
4 There *may / must* have been 600 statues on Easter Island.

b) Look at the statements again. How does the other verb change the meaning?

5  **Listen to check your answers to Exercise 4. Try saying the statements. Which words are stressed? Which words are contracted?**

6 <u>Underline</u> the modals which correctly complete the statements.

1 *must / can't / could / might have* + past participle = almost definitely happened
2 *must / can't / may have* + past participle = definitely did not happen (it was impossible)
3 *must / may / might / can't / could have* + past participle = possibly happened

7 a) Explain the difference between these two sentences.

1 It could have been John at the door.
2 It could be John at the door.

b) Decide which other modal verbs can be used to make present deductions.

Stonehenge

Practice

8 Read the facts about Mayan civilisation and make deductions using the verbs in brackets.

Example: We think the Mayan civilisation started in AD 250, but we can't be sure. It <u>might have begun</u> (begin) earlier.

1 No one knows why the civilisation ended. It _____ (be) because of an invasion or a war in which many Mayans were killed.
2 The Mayan people were experts in mathematics, created a system of writing and were excellent architects. They _____ (be) a very advanced society.
3 The wheel hadn't been invented when they were constructing their cities. They _____ (make) use of wheeled transport to move the stone.
4 We aren't certain why they cleared routes through the jungle. They _____ (trade) with neighbouring civilisations.
5 We know the Mayan civilisation existed independently and thrived for over three thousand years. They _____ (understand) how to farm the land and to organise their society.
6 There are a number of books and works of art which still exist from ancient times. Some of the Mayans _____ (be) well educated.
7 The Mayans wrote whole books with complex stories made from hieroglyphs (pictures with meanings). Only priests understood the whole language, so for most people, the books _____ (be) easy to read.

Get talking

9 In pairs, choose one of the following groups of people. Then discuss what life was like for these people in that place at that time. Think about food, places to live, religion, entertainment, work.

- settlers on Easter Island
- religious followers at Stonehenge thousands of years ago
- the Incas in Machu Picchu

In groups, talk about life in the area you discussed with your partner.

Language to go

A: It must have taken people ages to build that.
B: Yes, it can't have been an easy decision to knock it down.

> GRAMMAR REFERENCE PAGE 114
> PRACTICE PAGE 103

Vocabulary   Phrases for describing films
Function   Expressing reactions
Language to go   Giving your opinion

Film reviews

Speaking and vocabulary

1   **In pairs, discuss the following questions.**

1   How often do you go to the cinema?
2   Do you ever read film reviews?

2   **Complete the film review with words or phrases from the box.**

> storyline   performances   stars   location/setting
> direction   special effects   suspense   soundtrack
> script   supporting actors

Apart from the well-known **stars** in the movie, there were a number of good ¹ _____ , who also gave convincing ² _____ – perhaps we're looking at the stars of tomorrow! Most of the action is set on an island in the Pacific, a truly exotic ³ _____ , and the music was excellent – the ⁴ _____ was both memorable and atmospheric. A pity there wasn't an interesting ⁵ _____ – I would've got very bored indeed without the amazing ⁶ _____ . You could almost believe those monsters were real!

3   **In groups, discuss these questions.**

1   What makes a good film? Which of the features mentioned in Exercise 2 are important for you?
2   Can you think of films you have seen which have these qualities?
3   Do you recognise any of the films in the photos? Have you seen them? What did you think of them?

Listening

4   ▭ **Listen to two people talking about one of the films in the photos and answer the questions.**

1   Which film are they talking about?
2   Is their opinion of the film positive or negative?

5   **Listen again and make notes in the table on what the speakers say about each of the following categories.**

category	Charlotte	Daniel
general opinion		
acting		
storyline		
special effects		
soundtrack	—	
best part	—	

Language focus

6 Decide whether the phrases are positive (+), negative (–) or both (+/–) and mark each phrase accordingly. Use the recording script on page 121 to help you.

Example: It was absolutely brilliant. **+**

1 out of this world
2 breathtaking
3 It was worth every penny.
4 a real disappointment
5 I could hardly bear to watch.
6 … if you like that sort of thing.
7 It wasn't for me.
8 a bit over the top
9 I couldn't stand …
10 nothing special
11 overrated

Practice

7 Look at the sentences below and rewrite the phrases in *italics* using words or expressions from Exercise 6.

Example: It had excellent reviews, but *I don't think it was as good as they said*.
I think it was overrated.

1 It was so full of blood and guts – *I didn't want to look at the screen*.
2 It was fairly expensive, but *I really enjoyed it, so it didn't matter*.
3 I thought it would be better – it was *not as good as I was expecting*.
4 The special effects were … *they really took your breath away*.
5 The acting was *rather exaggerated and obvious*.
6 It was *really fantastic!*
7 *I really didn't like* the special effects.
8 On the whole, I thought *it wasn't really my kind of film*.

Get talking …

8 Prepare to describe a film you have seen. Think about what you are going to say. Make notes in the first column.

category	Your film Title:	Your partner's film Title:
general opinion		
acting		
storyline		
soundtrack		
special effects		
best part		

In pairs, talk about your films. Make notes on your partner's film in the second column.

… and writing

9 Use your notes to write a review of one of the films (120–180 words).

Language to go

A: Well, that was very overrated.
   A real disappointment.
B: Was it? I couldn't bear to watch.

> GRAMMAR REFERENCE PAGE 114
> PRACTICE PAGE 103

Vocabulary Phrases to describe machines
Grammar Future perfect/continuous
Language to go Talking about future developments in day-to-day living

Making life easier

Speaking and vocabulary

1 **Think of five gadgets or machines you use every day. Which is the most important to you?**

2 **Match the expressions with their opposites.**

1 It's *indispensable*.
2 It *saves me a lot of time*.
3 It *helps things run smoothly*.
4 It's *reliable*.

a) It's always *breaking down*.
b) It's *not very useful*.
c) It *wastes time*.
d) It's always *causing problems*.

3 **Describe a gadget or machine using these expressions.**

Example: My favourite machine is the washing machine! It saves me a lot of time, but when it breaks down, it causes problems.

4 **Look at the pictures with the article. In pairs, discuss the following.**

1 What do these inventions do?
2 Are they a good idea? Why? Why not?
3 What potential problems are there?

Reading

5 **Read the article to find the answers to the questions in Exercise 4.**

Grammar focus

6 **Look at this sentence and timeline and answer the questions.**

will + *have* + past participle
By the end of the decade, they **will have designed** a voice box that translates everything you say.

1 Will they design it before the end of the decade?
2 Do we know exactly when?

present   future

7 **Look at this sentence and timeline and answer the questions.**

will + *be* + *-ing*
Maybe in the near future, everyone **will be speaking** the same language.

1 Will the action be finished or still in progress in the future?
2 Will it happen just once or continuously?

present   future

AN EASIER LIFE FOR THE LAZY GENERATION

One potentially useful development is earphones that can translate foreign languages. You will be able to go to any country in the world and understand everything that's being said.

Of course, you won't be able to reply, although who knows? Maybe by the end of the decade, the inventors will have designed a voice box that translates everything you say. Or, on the other hand, maybe in the near future everyone will be speaking the same language anyway.

One machine that will definitely be speaking at least ten languages is the hot-pizza vendor that is being developed in Spain. This machine will be able to cook frozen pizzas in 90 seconds and, from its location in the street, it will call out in different languages to attract customers. I'm not sure what the quality of the pizza will be like, but no doubt dozens of scientists will have tried everything from the margherita to the calzone by the time the machine hits the streets.

A handy little gadget for the lazy gardener is the plant-waterer. This machine receives signals from the plant or flower when it is becoming too dry and then waters it as required. Of course, you need to remember to keep a tank full of water with the gadget. So, will our gardens be blooming beautifully after this invention? Maybe. Alternatively you could just move to a rainy country, like Britain.

Practice

8 **Match the questions with the answers and complete with the future simple (*will/won't*), future continuous or future perfect of the verbs in brackets.**

Example: Do you think you will still be working when you're 60?
No, I think I will have retired (retire) by then!

1 Will you be at home later?
2 Isn't the year 2070 too late for a cure for AIDS?
3 How will we be dealing with overcrowding at the end of the century?
4 Do you think travel will be easier in the future?
5 What will our great-great-grandchildren be doing in their free time?
6 Will all music be made by machines at the end of the century?
7 Can I have your homework by tomorrow at four o'clock, please?

a) Yes, we ______ (use) more powerful aeroplanes.
b) They ______ (play) virtual-reality games hour after hour, day after day.
c) People ______ (live) underground.
d) No. Composers ______ (find) new ways to keep their art alive by then.
e) Yes. The disease ______ (destroy) half the world by then.
f) Yes, that's fine. I ______ (finish) it by then.
g) Yes. I'll ______ (study) all evening because I have an exam tomorrow.

Get talking

9 **In groups, think of some gadgets or machines that would make your life easier. Think about:**

- who it would help
- possible problems
- whether the idea will really come into existence

Present your idea to the rest of the class.

Language to go

A: By the year 2050, they'll have invented a car that never breaks down.
B: Yes, but by then we won't be using cars any more.

> GRAMMAR REFERENCE PAGE 114
> PRACTICE PAGE 104

Vocabulary 1   Phrases for describing clothes
Vocabulary 2   Phrases for describing emotions
Language to go   Talking about your feelings

In a black mood

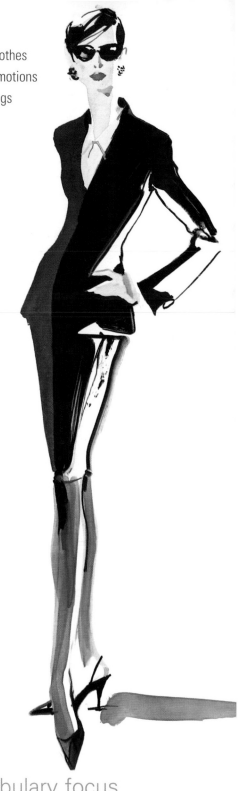

Speaking and vocabulary

1   In pairs, look at the pictures. Which style do you prefer? Tell your partner.

2   Put the words in the box into the correct columns.

> burgundy   a top   greeny-grey   scruffy   trainers   high heels
> plain   baggy   cream   fashionable   striped   tight-fitting
> smart   a suit   patterned   tights   reddish-brown

style	design	colour	fit	clothes/shoes
		burgundy		

3   In pairs, describe the pictures. What are they wearing?

4   In groups, discuss the following questions.

1   In general, what kinds of clothes do you prefer to wear? What does it depend on?
2   Do you choose particular colours for particular occasions?

Listening

5   💿 Listen to Emily, a colour therapist, and make notes on what she says.

colour	notes
violet	strong, creative; Leonardo ...
orange	
blue	
green	
red	
black	

Vocabulary focus

6   Match the words in *italics* with the phrases which best represent them.

Example: **1 c**

1   *inspired* and creative
2   *grumpy* and *in a bad mood*
3   depressed or *demotivated*
4   adventurous and *optimistic*
5   *a bit down* or feeling *lonely*
6   naturally *tranquil* temperament
7   feeling *restless*
8   tend to be rather *over-emotional*
9   *insecure* and in need of support
10   agitated and *nervous*

7 Look again at the words in *italics* in Exercise 6 and mark the stress on them. Listen to the words and repeat them.

Practice

8 **In pairs, look at the following situations and choose one or two words from Exercise 6 to describe how you would feel in each case.**

Example: You have just had a wonderful idea for a new project and you are sure your idea is original.
I'd feel inspired and nervous.

1 You have been doing the same job for years. Your boss and your colleagues show little respect for the work you do and your pay is rather low.
2 You are lying in a hammock by the beach listening to music and watching the sunset.
3 You have invited a special friend round to dinner. Absolutely everything is prepared and you have nothing left to do. You are feeling excited.
4 It's your first day in a new job and you are not sure if you are going to be able to do what is expected of you.
5 You oversleep, it's raining and your car breaks down on the way to work.
6 In the town where you are staying, very few people speak your language or English, and it is difficult to get a phone connection to call your friends.

9 **In pairs, choose three words from Exercise 6. Write situations for these words as in Exercise 8. Then, read your situations to another pair who will try to guess the feelings you describe.**

Get talking

10 **Look at the list and decide whether any of these factors affect your moods.**

- colours
- days of the week
- the weather
- your work
- your family
- money
- shopping
- clothes

In groups, discuss your ideas.

a) I can't keep still, and I've hardly slept.
b) I'm not sure that I can do it. I might need your help.
c) I've just had the most brilliant idea!
d) That's the most amazing thing I've ever heard! It makes me want to cry.
e) I keep worrying about my exams.
f) Just shut up, go away and leave me alone.
g) I can't be bothered to do it. I don't feel like it today.
h) Just relax. Take it easy.
i) Don't worry. Everything will be fine – you'll see.
j) Nothing seems to be going right at the moment. I wish someone else was here.

Language to go

A: I always feel happy and optimistic on a Friday, just before the weekend.
B: Me too, but then on Sundays I tend to feel a bit grumpy.

> PRACTICE PAGE 104

Vocabulary Verbs used for reporting
Grammar Constructions with reporting verbs
Language to go Giving other people's opinions

Missing the mark

Speaking

1 Look at these statements and tick (✔) the ones you agree with.

1 Brazil will win the next football World Cup.
2 In the future, every country in the world will use the same currency.
3 You will change your job in the next year.

2 Think of situations when we need to make predictions in our daily lives.

3 Look at the picture. What events and inventions are illustrated?

Listening and vocabulary

4 ▭ Listen to a radio programme about predictions which went completely wrong. As you listen, tick (✔) the topics mentioned.

sport cinema political matters dance
languages food computers transport

5 a) Listen again. Student A complete sentences 1–6 and Student B complete sentences 7–12.

Student A

1 Thomas J. Watson _____ that there was a world market for about five computers.
2 Bill Gates _____ that 640K on one computer would be enough for anybody.
3 Harry Warner _____ to see the potential of films with sound.
4 H.G. Wells _____ that he couldn't see submarines doing anything but suffocating their crew.
5 Lord Kelvin _____ that flying machines which were heavier than air were scientifically impossible.
6 Margaret Thatcher _____ in 1969 that no woman in her time would be Prime Minister.

Student B

7 Ken Olson calmly _____ the World Future Society that there was no reason for any individual to have a computer in their home.
8 Charlie Chaplin _____ us that cinema was just a passing fashion.
9 The co-founder of Rolls Royce _____ the world that he didn't think flights across the Atlantic were possible.
10 Lord Kelvin _____ that the radio had no future.
11 Lord Kelvin _____ that X-rays were possible.
12 Ronald Reagan _____ that there wasn't a word for 'freedom' in the Russian language.

b) In pairs, complete all the sentences.

Grammar focus

6 Write the verbs from Exercise 5 next to their structure and definition.

- **verb (+ *that*)**

  <u>announce</u> make something known publicly

  <u>claim</u> say something is real or true

  1 _____ indicate

  2 _____ express a strong belief (often repeatedly) especially when others do not believe you

  3 _____ make a guess about the future

  4 _____ say that a statement isn't true

  5 _____ try to prove something by giving reasons

- **verb (+ object + *that*)**

  6 _____ make someone aware of a danger

  7 _____ cause to feel certain/show that you are confident of something

- **verb (+ *that*) or (+ *to* + gerund)**

  8 _____ admit something negative (e.g. guilt for a crime)

- **verb (+ *to* + infinitive)**

  9 _____ not accept (to do) something

- **verb (+ *to* + infinitive) or (+ *that*) or (+ object + *that*)**

  10 _____ guarantee something/be completely certain

Practice

7 Report these sentences using the words or phrases in *italics*.

Example: Nuclear energy will never be attainable. (Albert Einstein, 1932) *announce*
Einstein announced that nuclear energy would never be attainable.

1 The English are bad soldiers, and we will settle the matter by lunchtime. (Napoleon, before the Battle of Waterloo, 1815) *assure his generals*

2 There is not much demand for animal stories in the USA. (Dial Press rejecting George Orwell's *Animal Farm*, 1944) *point out*

3 Nicotine is a very remarkable and good drug. (Sir Charles Effis, scientist, 1962) *insist*

4 Everything that can be invented has been invented. (US Commissioner of Patents, 1899) *claim*

5 Rock and roll will be gone by June. (*Variety* Newspaper, 1955) *promise*

6 Space travel is impossible. (Dr Richard van der Riet Woolley, astronomer, 1956) *deny*

7 The brain is an organ of minor importance. (Aristotle, Greek philosopher, 4th century BC) *argue*

8 Bill Clinton will lose. (The *Wall Street Journal*, commenting on the 1996 Presidential election, 1995) *predict*

Get talking

8 Look at these statements. Choose one you feel strongly about and discuss it briefly with a partner.

- Travel is the best form of education.
- Technology has made the world a better place.
- Space travel is a waste of money.
- All public transport should be free.

Change partners after two minutes. Report your first partner's opinions. What did they claim/insist/argue etc.? Discuss another topic and change partners again.

Language to go

A: You assured me that the experiment wasn't dangerous!
B: No, I warned you that it might be.

> GRAMMAR REFERENCE PAGE 114

> PRACTICE PAGE 105

Vocabulary   Types of books
Grammar   Participles in narratives
Language to go   Telling stories

Now or never

Vocabulary and speaking

1   Answer these questions.

1   Have you read any detective
novels or seen any films involving
detectives?
2   What qualities do detectives need?

**2   Look at these types of books and
answer the question.**

> manual   encyclopaedia
> cook book   guidebook   biography
> autobiography   diary   thriller
> volume of poetry

Which of these books do you need if
you want to …?

1   find some information about the
world in general
2   find out about a holiday destination
3   read an exciting (and not true)
story
4   find an interesting recipe
5   read all about a famous person (in
his/her own words)
6   read about a famous person (in
someone else's words)
7   find out how to use your machine
8   write about your daily life
9   read something beautifully written
in few words

3   In pairs, discuss these questions.

1   Which type of book do you think
the extract on the right comes
from?
2   What do you think happens in the
extract?

Reading

**4   Read the extract from a detective
story, *Harley's Ghost*, to see if you
were right.**

Harley sat in his car.
Watching, waiting. With each
passing hour, he knew the
chance to catch his man was
fading fast. As dawn broke
and the traffic grew noisier, he
started to fall asleep. By the
time the sound of a car horn
woke him suddenly, the city
had come alive – a million
moving bodies, maybe hiding
the one that really mattered.
Opening the car door, Harley
felt the cold autumn wind
biting into his skin and he
knew that he had to go in.

'Now or never,' he said to
himself. 'Waiting can drive a
man crazy and I'm too young
to go crazy.'

Knowing it was his only
chance, he cautiously
approached the steps of the
tall, grey building. He pushed
at the door, slowly, and to his
surprise, it opened. Taking
one step, he found himself in
a dark corridor. No sound.
No voices. Just his own heart
beating heavily. If K was in
there, he would be on the
second floor. Harley took the
steps one by one, feeling for
the gun in the deep pocket of
his coat. When he reached the
top, he stopped dead still. It
was nothing he could see or
hear, but there in the gloom,
in that deadly silence, he felt
someone watching him.

Grammar focus

5 Look at the different uses of these participle expressions from the extract and find others in the text. In which way is each one used?

1 To describe when two actions happen at the same time.
Opening the car door, Harley felt …

2 To give the reason for an action.
Knowing it was his only chance, he cautiously approached the steps.

3 As adjectives (or as 'reduced' relative clauses).
With each *passing* hour, …

4 As nouns.
Waiting can drive a man crazy.

5 After many verbs of sensation (verb + object + -ing): *see*, *feel*, *watch*, *hear* etc.
He felt someone *watching* him.

Practice

6 Rewrite the continuation of Harley's story, using participles to keep the meaning the same.

Example: He turned round and saw an old lady who was sweeping the floor.
Turning round, he saw an old lady sweeping the floor.

1 He used a credit card to break in, and he checked the room on the second floor.

2 The room was empty, but he felt the wind which was blowing through the open window.

3 It told him that someone had been there recently and escaped, and ripped their trousers at the same time.

4 While he searched for clues, he found a receipt for a plane ticket to Hawaii.

5 Because he realised he had to get to the airport quickly, he jumped into his car.

6 Thirty minutes later, Harley ran into the airport and saw the crowds which were waiting in lines.

Get talking …

7 In pairs, look at the pictures and work out what happens at the end of the story. Describe it to your partner.

… and writing

8 Using participles where appropriate, write the final part of the story in 120–180 words.

Language to go

A: I see you're working late again, officer.
B: Catching criminals is my favourite game, sir.

> GRAMMAR REFERENCE PAGE 115
> PRACTICE PAGE 105

The dream business

Speaking and listening

1 In groups, discuss these questions.

   1 Do you use the Internet regularly?

   2 Do you know of any businesses which operate only on the Internet?

   3 Would you like to have your own Internet company? Why / Why not?

2 🔲 **Listen to the Jazz Editor at www.musicmaker.com and answer these questions.**

   1 How big is the company's jazz section?

   2 How does he describe his general role (what he does for www.musicmaker.com's customers)?

   3 Is he only interested in the most famous jazz musicians?

   4 Who sends him e-mails?

   5 What negative points does he mention about his job?

3 **In groups, discuss whether you would use www.musicmaker.com.**

Grammar focus

4 Put the correct prepositions with these words.

Responsibility	**Organisation / Solving problems**
1 be ____ charge ____	7 deal ____
2 be responsible ____	8 cope ____
3 take care ____	9 sort ____

Focus	**Other**
4 be concerned ____	10 liaise ____
5 specialise ____	11 depend ____
6 concentrate ____	12 resign ____
	13 invest ____
	14 be proud ____
	15 consist ____

5 Match the phrases from Exercise 4 with the correct definitions.

a) have control over a particular aspect/part
b) look after
c) have total control over something

d) focus on a single aim
e) be worried about
f) train in/focus on one particular subject

g) manage a situation successfully
h) put into a logical order
i) take action on something

j) put money into a project and expect a profit
k) give up a job
l) communicate and maintain contact with
m) be made/formed of
n) be influenced/determined by something *or* rely on someone/something
o) be pleased or satisfied with something connected to yourself (possessions, abilities etc.)

Practice

6 Complete the letter with prepositional phrases from Exercise 4.

Dear Mr Forbes,

Thank you for your interest. Below are details of our business plan.
Our new restaurant will _specialise in_ Mongolian food. Though I will be ¹ _____ the day-to-day running of the restaurant, the staff will ² _____ a team of six, including the head waiter and head chef, ³ _____ the cooking. Several local companies have already ⁴ _____ the business, though their future investment will ⁵ _____ our profits in the first year. There are already two restaurants in the area, but we believe we can ⁶ _____ the competition. In the last year, we have ⁷ _____ local community leaders, who were at first ⁸ _____ possible problems about parking. This has now been ⁹ _____ , and they are, at present, very keen on our plans.
We look forward to hearing from you soon.

Yours sincerely,
James Smith

Get talking ...

7 Imagine you could set up any company you wanted.

1 What product/service would you offer?
2 What would it be called?

8 In groups, talk about your ideas and choose one of them. Discuss the following aspects, then present your proposal to the class.

- Where would your head office be?
- How many people would work there?
- What would your responsibilities be?
- How would you work together?
- What would the market be for your product?
- How would you attract new business?

... and writing

9 Write a profile of your company, explaining its focus, organisation and workers' responsibilities.

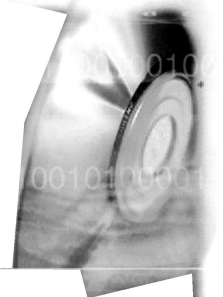

Language to go

A: Can you tell me a little bit about your company?
B: It consists of ten people and we specialise in evening wear.

> GRAMMAR REFERENCE PAGE 115
> PRACTICE PAGE 106

Vocabulary   Body idioms
Language to go   Using idiomatic English

Fingers crossed

Speaking and reading

1   In pairs, discuss what is happening in the pictures.

2   Look at the pictures again. Each one illustrates an English idiom containing a different part of the body. Do you know what they are?

3   Read the article and check your answers.

4   Discuss whether you have similar idioms in your language.

Seeing eye to eye with English

OK, let's face facts: English is not an easy language. As well as its irregularities and enormous lists of rules, it has thousands of tricky idioms – too many to learn by heart. And what do they all mean? Sometimes you can only guess and keep your fingers crossed. Take these bodily examples:

Little children are often called 'cheeky'. Why? Because they are rude to adults. But surely they don't use their cheeks to be rude? And what about nosy old women? Have they got lots of noses? No, they are interested in everyone else's business and of course they will get on your nerves after a while.

If you're busy at work, you probably have your hands full, though actually it's your desk that will be full. And if you let things get out of hand, you may need someone to give you a hand so that you don't get the elbow. But on the other hand, if you see eye to eye with your boss, you'll probably keep your job anyway.

Even out of the workplace you can't escape idioms. Imagine you go to a restaurant. First you have to catch the waiter's eye to get a menu. Then you have to make up your mind about what to eat.

All these idioms – it's enough to break your heart!

Vocabulary focus

5 Find 'body' idioms in the text to match these meanings.

Fingers and hands
Example: make a gesture of good luck
keep your fingers crossed
1 be extremely busy
2 become too difficult to control
3 help someone
4 in contrast

Heart
5 memorise information very well
6 make someone feel extremely sad

Eye
7 agree with someone (generally or about one specific subject)
8 attract someone's attention

Other parts of the head
9 confront the truth
10 disrespectful (especially children)
11 too interested in the private matters of people around you
12 decide

Other parts of the body
13 annoy someone
14 be fired from a job

Practice

6 Rewrite these sentences with the words in brackets so that they mean the same, using idioms from Exercise 5. Write between two and five words in each space.

Example: It's not always easy to choose which film to see in big cinemas.
It's sometimes difficult to **make up your mind** about which film to see in cinemas. (make)

1 His secretary helped him to do the job.
   His secretary _____ . (hand)
2 Memorising facts isn't always the best way.
   Learning things _____ could sometimes be counterproductive. (by)
3 Unless we take special precautions, the party could get out of control.
   The party might _____ if we aren't careful. (out)
4 Despite John jumping and waving for ten minutes, the waiter still didn't see him.
   John jumped and waved for ten minutes but he still _____ . (catch)
5 I had found the music annoying long before she switched it off.
   The music had _____ for some time before she switched it off. (nerves)
6 Wish me luck for my exam today.
   _____ for me today in my exam. (keep)
7 We never shared the same opinions about anything.
   We didn't _____ about anything. (to)
8 That's true, but – to give the opposite view – men and women are not physically equal.
   You're right, but _____ men and women are physically unequal. (on)

Get talking

7 In groups, discuss these questions.

1 What things in English do you think you need to learn by heart?
2 What/Who gets on your nerves?
3 Do you know any nosy people? If so, how do you react to them?
4 When was the last time you made up your mind to do something important (for example, change job, learn English)?
5 What type of person do you see eye to eye with?
6 When was the last time you gave someone a hand? When were you last given a hand?

Language to go

A: Do you see eye to eye with your neighbour?
B: Not really. She's a bit too nosy.

> PRACTICE PAGE 106

Vocabulary   Phrasal verbs for describing opportunities
Grammar   *Should have/if only/wish* + past perfect
Language to go   Talking about regrets and missed opportunities

I wish ...

Speaking and vocabulary

1   **Find the phrasal verbs in the questions below to match these definitions.**

down	**out**
1 refuse	5 not take advantage
2 be disappointed	of an opportunity
	6 begin a journey

up	**off**
3 stop a habit	7 delay
4 register	8 happen

Have you ever ...

* *turned down* an invitation to a really good party?
* *given up* doing something you really enjoyed?
* *missed out* on an opportunity to meet someone you admired?
* *put something off* until it was too late?
* been *let down* by a good friend?
* *signed up* for a course, and then decided you didn't want to do it?
* *set out* on a long journey and then realised you have left something important behind?
* made plans with someone, which never *came off*?

2   **In pairs, ask each other the questions.**

3   **Look at the photos, which represent four 'missed opportunities'. In pairs, discuss what you think each one was about.**

Listening and speaking

4   🔲 **Listen to the four people telling their stories. Were you right?**

5   **Re-tell the stories to your partner. Check with the recording script on page 122 if necessary.**

6   a) 🔲 **Listen again and, when you hear the 'beep', decide which two sentences can be used to finish each story.**

1   *I wish he'd* retired earlier.
2   *I wish I'd stayed* with the band.
3   *If only I hadn't* panicked.
4   *If only I hadn't* been so shy.
5   *I should have asked* him for his autograph.
6   *I should've waited* another year.
7   *I shouldn't have* turned him down.
8   *I shouldn't have* taken this job.

b) **Discuss which of the stories you think is the biggest 'missed opportunity'.**

Practice

8 **Complete the dialogues using *should have*, *if only* or *I wish.***

Example: A: I don't believe it!
        B: What's wrong?
        A: We've been burgled! **If only** I hadn't left the window open.

1 A: Oh, no, I've burnt the pie!
     B: How did you manage that?
     A: I fell asleep.
     B: Perhaps you _____ .
2 A: I was there at the top of this mountain, with my camera.
     B: Fantastic.
     A: But then I realised I'd run out of film.
     B: Oh, how annoying! I bet you _____ .
3 A: How was the holiday?
     B: A disaster. We lost all our luggage, and we don't have any insurance. I wish _____ .
4 A: So he split up with Sarah, who was lovely, and married Elaine, who was awful. And then they got divorced after two terrible years.
     B: Poor man! If _____ .
5 A: All my flowers have died. I can't understand it.
     B: Did you water them?
     A: Yes, every two months.
     B: Maybe you _____ .
6 A: Have you decided which flights to get yet?
     B: Yes, and I've bought the tickets, but they were more expensive than last week.
     A: Oh, I knew we _____ .

9 🎧 **Listen to the examples on the recording. What happens to the sounds *have* and *had*? Practise saying the sentences using the contractions *'ve* and *'d*.**

Get talking and writing

10 **In groups, prepare to take part in a radio show.**

- Read about your missed opportunity.
- Invent the details to complete the story.
- Write the final sentence(s) using the prompt given.
- Tell your story to your group. Can they guess the ending?

Student A: Turn to page 85.
Student B: Turn to page 86.
Student C: Turn to page 85.

Language to go

A: Perhaps I should have asked you before inviting everyone round.
B: I wish you had. If only I'd known!

Grammar focus

7 **a) Look at these sentences from the stories and choose the correct forms to complete the constructions.**

I *shouldn't have turned* him *down*.
I *should have asked* him for his autograph.
If only I *hadn't* been so shy.
I *wish* I*'d stayed* with the band.

1 should(n't) have + *infinitive / past perfect / past participle*
2 wish + *infinitive / past perfect / past participle*
3 if only + *infinitive / past perfect / past participle*

b) Answer the questions.

1 Which construction is used to blame or criticise someone?
2 Which two are used to express strong personal regrets?

> GRAMMAR REFERENCE PAGE 115
> PRACTICE PAGE 107

Mind your manners

Reading and speaking

1 Do the questionnaire below.
In pairs, compare your answers.

Listening

2 Listen to people in the same
situations. What do they do? Tick (✔)
a), b) or c) for each one.

How polite *are you?*

1 You are in a bar
on your own,
enjoying a book,
when someone
comes over and
asks if they can sit
at your table. Do
you …?

a smile and offer
him/her a seat
b tell him/her to
get lost
c keep looking at
your book

2 Your brother-in-law and his family (three screaming kids
and pets) have just visited you. It was awful. When they
leave do you …?

a stand by the car smiling and thank them for a
wonderful weekend
b wish them a good
journey and invite
them to come and
stay again soon
c tell them this was
the worst weekend
of your life and
that you hope they
never set foot in
your house again

3 Your best friend has just passed her
driving test at the fifth attempt. Do
you …?

a congratulate her and open a
bottle of champagne
b ask her how on earth she
managed to do it
c explain to her that in that case
you won't be giving her any more
lifts to work in the future

4 A group of good friends has organised a trip to the theatre and has asked you to go. You have heard that the play is not particularly good. Do you …?

a tell them that the play is rubbish and you wouldn't dream of going

b tell them what you have heard and suggest going to see something else

c keep quiet and go to see it anyway

5 You are in a restaurant and the waiter spills a glass of red wine down your new shirt. Do you …?

a tell him/her she is a complete idiot and shouldn't be allowed to work in a restaurant

b act as if nothing had happened

c accept the apology (after all, it was an accident)

Language focus

3 Look at the phrases from the dialogues. What is their function? Match the headings with the groups of phrases.

- Responding to thanks
- Giving good/bad news
- Apologising
- Inviting **1**
- Responding to an invitation

- Responding to an apology
- Saying goodbye
- Thanking someone
- Responding to good/bad news

| 1 | Do you fancy -ing?
How about -ing?
Can I get you a …? | 2 | That'd be lovely.
That's very kind, but …
Thank you for the offer, but …
I'd love to.
Thank you anyway. |

| 3 | You'll never guess what …
I'm afraid … | 4 | Brilliant!
I'm sorry to hear that.
Well done! Congratulations!
How awful! |

| 5 | It was really kind of you to …
Thank you so much for -ing. | 6 | Not at all.
It's a pleasure.
You're welcome. |

| 7 | I'm sorry, but I've …
I'm afraid …
Sorry about that. | 8 | That's all right/fine.
Don't worry about it.
It's no problem (at all). |

| 9 | It was lovely to meet you.
Good to see you again.
Have a good trip!
See you again soon.
See you, then. |

Practice

4 🔲 Listen to the dialogues again and reply with a suitable expression. Use the recording script on page 122.

5 In pairs, practise the dialogues.

Get talking

6 Play the game 'What do you say when …?' Turn to pages 85 and 87.

Language to go

A: You'll never guess what …
B: What?
A: I've finished *Language to go*!
B: Congratulations!

> GRAMMAR REFERENCE PAGE 115

> PRACTICE PAGE 107

Information for pair and group work

Lesson 6, Exercise 4, Student A

Richard Burton and Liz Taylor

The famous British actor, Richard Burton, saw Liz Taylor for the first time at a party in California. They got on well and later worked together on a film called *Cleopatra* before getting married. Fame came quickly, but at the expense of their relationship: they got divorced in 1974. However, they made up, got back together and remarried the following year. But in the media spotlight, they couldn't get over the problems involved in being one of the world's most glamorous couples, and their second marriage didn't last. They divorced again after just a few months.

Lesson 19, Exercise 6, Student A

Chipuru Bojanna was an Indian living in Dubai who earned a tiny salary collecting boxes. He hadn't seen his family for three years because he couldn't afford to fly home. He finished work at six o'clock every day. One day he:
- found a wallet containing £2,000 at 5.55 in the afternoon;
- thought, 'Shall I keep the money or be honest?';
- noticed the owner's name in the wallet;
- looked him up in the telephone book;
- told owner '… nearly kept the money … nearly bought ticket to India';
- returned the wallet to owner, who gave him a reward.

Lesson 22, Exercise 3, Student A

Tokyo

Kate: Tokyo is easy to *get around*. You can *take the subway* to most areas of the city. It's cheap, easy to use and clean, compared to London.

In the main commercial parts, the Japanese are very smart, while the younger generation is fashionable; their freedom to wear what they like is *taken for granted*. Walking in the parks, you might see a few buskers, and there are sometimes long queues of women waiting to *get their palms read* by a fortune teller.

My favourite park is called Hibiya. You *get* rollerbladers and kids on kickboards, and, from what I saw, quite a lot of flirting *takes place* between boys and girls here.

In Shinjuku there are a lot of homeless people living in 'damboll' which are like cardboard boxes. Many of these boxes are covered in striking graffiti. That's another thing you *get to know* about the Japanese – they are a very artistic people and they are brilliant designers.

Lesson 28, Exercise 8, Student A

ACROSS
1 *an insect which hops*
4
7
9
10
13
14
17
19
20
21
22

Lesson 31, Exercise 3, Student A

Stonehenge

Built in prehistoric times (3000–1600 BC), Stonehenge has 80 blocks altogether, organised into a circle and a horseshoe. The biggest of the stones are seven metres tall and weigh around 50 tonnes. No one knows how the stones were placed here, but they must have been transported from South Wales to the site, nearly 300 kilometres away, and it must have taken about 600 people to move each stone. One theory is that they could have floated the stones across a river. Why was it built? It's likely to have been a meeting place for tribes, or a religious centre, or it may even have been a type of early calendar. There is still a sun-worshipping festival here to celebrate Midsummer's Day, 21st June.

Lesson 12, Exercise 10

Pasta with chicken and tomato
Ingredients:
chopped tomatoes
some garlic
two chicken breasts
an onion
pasta
parmesan cheese

Chop the onions and garlic into small pieces. Fry the chicken on a medium heat, turning once. After eight minutes, add the onions and garlic. Mix them. Add the chopped tomatoes, stirring occasionally. Let the mixture simmer. Bring a large pan of water to boil and add the pasta. When the pasta is ready, drain it and pour the sauce over the pasta. Add some parmesan cheese, allowing it to melt. Serve immediately.

Lesson 17, Exercise 4

KEY

If you chose mainly **a**
Lucky you! You always look on the bright side of life! The future looks good.

If you chose mainly **b**
Cheer up and stop being so miserable. Things aren't as bad as you think, and they won't get any better until you change your outlook a little.

If you chose mainly **c**
You are very level headed and logical. There won't be any surprises for you tomorrow.

Lesson 31, Exercise 3, Student C

Machu Picchu

This ruined city in Peru was discovered in 1911 by the American explorer Hiram Bingham. It's situated at the top of a mountain, nearly 600 metres above the Urubamba River. This means the air is very thin, and it can be difficult for tourists to breathe. The city is a mass of staircases, climbing up to the temples, palaces, towers and fountains. We know very little about its history, but the city may have been built by the Incas from Cuzco, as a place to hide from Spanish invaders in the 15th century.

Lesson 39, Exercise 10, Student C

A friend bought you some tickets for a concert. (What concert?)
These were a present. (What for?)
You arranged to meet your friend on the evening of the concert. (Where?)
Your friend didn't arrive, but you waited. As a result, you arrived late and you weren't allowed in. (How did you feel?)

Finish the story with a sentence:
- I wish I'd …
- I should have …
- I shouldn't have …
- If only I had …

Lesson 40, Exercise 6

WHAT DO YOU SAY WHEN …?
See page 87 for game board.
- Play this game in groups of four (A+B+C+D), working in two pairs (A+B and C+D).
- You will need a different-coloured counter each. Place your counters on the start.
- The object of the game is to reach your role-play arrow before the other pair.
- Move in the order A, B, C, D.
- To move, put your counter on the next square for your letter (player A moves to the next 'A' square, etc.), read the situation and respond appropriately. Your partner can help you.
- If you make a mistake, go back to where you were, and wait for your next turn, when you can try again.
- When you both reach your role-play card, read it and then act out the situation to the other pair. When both pairs have done their role-plays, decide which pair was the most polite!

Lesson 39, Exercise 10, Student A

You were going to play for your country. (Which sport?)
It was an important match. (Which match?)
One week before the match, you had an accident. (What happened?)
As a result, you weren't able to play, but the team won the championship. (How did you feel?)

Finish the story with a sentence:
- I wish I'd …
- I should have …
- I shouldn't have …
- If only I had …

Lesson 6, Exercise 4, Student B

Nelson and Winnie Mandela

Winnie Madikizela first came across Nelson Mandela when she saw him in a law court. At that time, he was a lawyer. Soon afterwards, they met in a café and took to each other immediately. They got married in 1958. By then, Nelson was already fighting against apartheid. Denounced as a terrorist, he went to prison in 1964. While he was in prison, Winnie carried on his work for the ANC (African National Congress). Nelson was finally released after 26 years in prison, and with elections now open to all, he became President of South Africa. But Winnie and Nelson fell out over political and personal differences, and they split up. Nelson married his third wife, Gracia Machel, in 1998.

Lesson 19, Exercise 6, Student B

Fifteen English work colleagues put their money into a lottery together every week. They always bet on the same numbers, and their organiser was supposed to put the collected money on the lottery. Eventually their numbers appeared and …

- they … win £128,000 each, but they won nothing;
- the organiser had never entered the lottery (he had kept their money every week);
- one unlucky loser said, 'It's terrible. I … to quit my job and buy a new house … but now it's impossible';
- another: '… buy a boat with the money and sail around the world';
- the organiser was suspended from work because angry colleagues … (about) attack him.

Lesson 22, Exercise 3, Student B

London

Mikako: It's important to *take advantage of* the sights and sounds of the London streets. It doesn't take long to *get to* the centre, where most of the tourist attractions are found, because you can *take the Tube*.

The saddest thing about the street life is the number of homeless people you *get* in the centre. This *took me by surprise* because London is such a wealthy city. But there were many happier sights too.

For real London street life, have a look at any of the markets – Camden, Portobello Road or Spitalfields and also Covent Garden, where you can find magicians, street vendors, fire-eaters and buskers. *Take your time* and *get to know* these places. They do *get crowded*, but they're worth visiting.

The fashion is incredible. People wear anything they want, and no one *takes any notice*. All the different styles are *taken for granted*.

Lesson 28, Exercise 8, Student B

DOWN

2 the season which comes after winter	12
3	14
5	15
6	16
8	18
11	19

Lesson 31, Exercise 3, Student B

Easter Island statues

Who made these amazing stone heads and why? Carved from soft volcanic rock, they consist of huge heads with extra long ears and noses. They vary in size from three to twelve metres high. One belief is that the people who came to the island nearly eighteen centuries ago were South Americans and might have built them as a depiction of their gods. Today, there are about 100 statues left standing on the island, but in the past there may have been as many as 600.

Lesson 39, Exercise 10, Student B

Your grandparents lived through an important time in your country. (What happened?)
They died when you were young. (How old were you?)
They loved talking about their experiences but you were too young to understand. (What were their experiences?)
Now you are a reporter and you would like to write about their stories. (Who do you work for?)

Finish the story with a sentence:
- I wish I'd …
- I should have …
- I shouldn't have …
- If only I had …

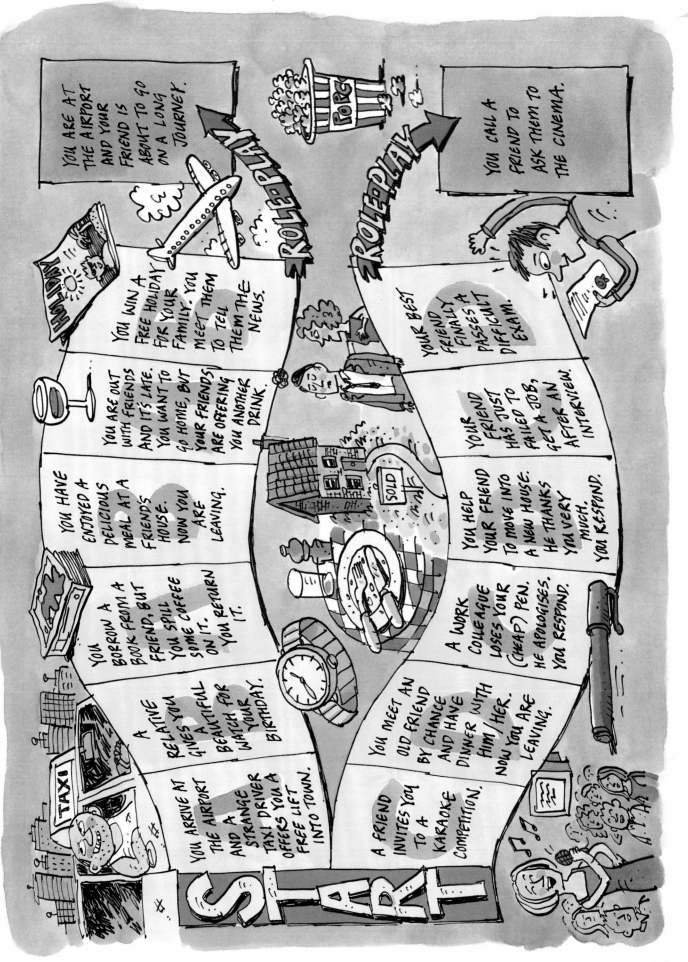

Practice

1 Getting ahead

Vocabulary: phrases for talking about your life

1 Use the phrases in the box to complete the sentences. You may need to change the tense.

> be into   achieve your goal(s)   take up
> be lucky enough to   do (something) for a living
> sacrifice   broaden your horizons

Example: Spending time in another country can be a great way to **broaden your horizons**.

1 Recently I _____ photography as a hobby.
2 I've always _____ jazz.
3 We had to _____ going on holiday when we were saving to buy a house.
4 'What do you _____?' 'I'm a receptionist.'
5 After years of hard training, she finally _____ of playing at Wimbledon.
6 They _____ meet each other at university.

Grammar: review of tenses

2 Correct the mistakes in the following sentences.

Example: I really ~~am loving~~ speaking English with my friends. ✗ *love*

1 I have been to Brazil last summer. It was wonderful.
2 This evening, I go out to dinner in a small, local restaurant.
3 I am always enjoying eating good food.
4 In my life, I went travelling many times.
5 I am meeting people every day through my work.
6 I've started studying English when I was at school.
7 I was meeting him when I lived in Asia.
8 This weekend I go to see an art exhibition.

3 Read the following two interviews and complete the sentences by putting the verbs in brackets in the correct form.

Example: When **did** you first **get into** sculpture? (get into)

A

1 I _____ when I _____ at school. (start / be)
2 I _____ a wonderful teacher who _____ me. (have / inspire)
3 I _____ always _____ playing with strange objects, since I _____ very young. (love / be)
4 _____ you _____ any major successes? (have)
5 Last year, I _____ an award, and next month I _____ my work at a gallery in Prague. (win / show)

B

6 _____ you always _____ cooking? (enjoy)
7 Not really. I _____ in Italy when it first _____ an obsession. (live / become)
8 _____ you _____ any plans to do it for a living? (have)
9 I _____ as a chef at the moment, to get some experience. (work)
10 Then I think I _____ my own restaurant. I've been saving up to buy the right place. (open)

2 Modern survival

Vocabulary: health and lifestyles

1 Complete the sentences using adjectives with the same meaning as the prompts in brackets.

1 I enjoy my work, but it is _____ . (very tiring)
2 At the end of the day, I find going to the gym very _____ . (helps me to feel less stressed)
3 I love going to the countryside – the air is so _____ ! (opposite of dirty)
4 I find life in a big city like Tokyo too _____ . (makes you anxious)
5 All those cars mean the city is very _____ . (full of fumes)
6 I really should eat less fast food – my diet is very _____ . (bad for you)

2 Complete the dialogues with words or phrases from the lesson. You will have to change the tenses.

Example: A: Have another biscuit.
B: No, thanks, I'm trying to **watch my weight**.

1 A: He still smokes about 40 a day!
   B: Yeah, but it used to be 60, so at least he has _____ .
2 A: Look at my muscles!
   B: Wow! Have you been _____ ?
3 A: We've got a big match on Sunday, so we've been training hard.
   B: Really? And are you _____ ?
4 A: Do you still do Tai Chi?
   B: No, I _____ it _____ .
5 A: The doctor told me to eat more fruit and vegetables and less fast food.
   B: You mean he doesn't think you have a _____ diet?
6 A: I tried this Shiatsu massage.
   B: Oh, yes? What does that do?
   A: Well, it's very good for _____ .
7 A: I feel terrible.
   B: Why?
   A: I'm supposed to be on a diet, but I'm eating more than usual and I've actually _____ on _____ !

3 <u>Underline</u> the correct option to complete the text.

MIND AND BODY

I rely on a healthy mind to keep my body *exhausting / ~~in good shape~~ / worked out*. I try not to lead a very [1] *polluted / cut down / stressful* life, or spend too much time in busy, [2] *polluted / healthy / stress-free* cities. I might do some exercise, but I'd rather [3] *relieved stress / give up / work out* on the beach than in the gym, and not after work – that's too [4] *unhealthy / relaxing / exhausting*! At the end of a long day, I would rather do something [5] *exhausting / stressful / relaxing*. And if I had to [6] *watch my weight / give up / cut down on* something, it would be the number of hours I work, rather than the food I enjoy. I have a fairly [7] *balanced diet / healthy / work out* because I eat a lot of different food, but I [8] *gave up / cut down / was in good shape* watching my weight years ago.

3 Coincidences

Vocabulary: time adverbials

1 Complete the sentences with words or phrases from the box which mean the same as the words in brackets.

as soon as eventually lately later often previously simultaneously whenever

1 Both lectures are being held _____ . (at the same time)
2 I'll give you a call _____ . (afterwards)
3 _____ it rains, she arrives ten minutes late. (every time)
4 The information had been sent _____ . (before)
5 They _____ managed to find the key. (in the end)
6 Have you heard from Rob _____ ? (recently)
7 I _____ meet her on my way to work. (frequently)
8 We came _____ we heard the news. (immediately)

Grammar: narrative tenses

2 Complete the story using the correct tense of the verbs in brackets.

Shock in the Desert
I ¹ _____ (live) in Egypt for about six months when I decided I needed a holiday. Cairo is a pretty congested place, and what I ² _____ (want) was a bit of peace and quiet. So I ³ _____ (decide) to head off to the desert, to a little oasis called Farafra. I got straight on the bus. A friend ⁴ _____ (tell) me that I wouldn't need to book my seat.

We ⁵ _____ (travel) for about twelve hours when I saw this incredibly beautiful little oasis. As I ⁶ _____ (expect) from my friend's description, it had lovely palm trees, very few tourists, great food and it was quiet, totally different from the city.

I ⁷ _____ (stay) there for a couple of days when I ⁸ _____ (get) the shock of my life. It was late afternoon and I ⁹ _____ (have) a shower when suddenly I caught sight of something out of the corner of my eye. It was something on the wall. I turned to look and I ¹⁰ _____ (see) this massive scorpion.

I just screamed and ¹¹ _____ (jump) out of the shower. I managed to put on a towel, and after I ¹² _____ (calm down), I picked up my shoe and returned to the shower. While the scorpion ¹³ _____ (crawl) up the wall, I took aim and ¹⁴ _____ (hit) it with my shoe. It was only a lot later that I realised I ¹⁵ _____ (never be) so scared in all my life.

The strangest thing was that when I ¹⁶ _____ (get back) to Cairo, I ¹⁷ _____ (discover) that my flatmate ¹⁸ _____ (go) to hospital. She ¹⁹ _____ (find) a scorpion in the flat and it ²⁰ _____ (sting) her!

4 Friends

Vocabulary: noun combinations with -*friend* and -*mate*

1 Complete the following dialogues with suitable words or phrases.

Example: I can't imagine ever losing touch with Matthew. We are complete <u>soulmates</u>.

1 If you can't remember what your homework is, why don't you call one of your _____ ?
2 I always go out on a Friday night with a group of _____ . It is nice to be able to socialise after a busy week at work.
3 I don't like the way my _____ never pays the rent on time, because I always have to apologise to our landlady.
4 I have a _____ in China. We have never met, but we have always written a lot, and now we e-mail each other every week.
5 Angela is in a very good mood these days. Do you think it is because of her new _____ ?
6 Philip is such a _____ . He's only ever interested in going out and having a good time, and disappears as soon as there is a problem to sort out.

Grammar: phrases of addition, result and contrast

2 <u>Underline</u> the correct option.

1 We should finish the report today, *because of this / although / as well as* it might be worth waiting until tomorrow for the last results to come in.
2 He was always late for work and *as well as / on the other hand / as a result* he lost his job.
3 I try to have a healthy social life *despite / however / because of this* playing sport and working long hours *too / as well as / therefore*.
4 I really get on well with my workmates and we share the same interests. *Although / Because of this / However*, we do tend to talk about work a bit too much.
5 I love having friends to stay in the house. *Too / On the other hand / Therefore*, when they stay for more than a week, it can be exhausting!

3 Rewrite the following sentences using a linking word or phrase from the box.

because of this   as a result   on the other hand although   nevertheless   also   therefore

Example: It was raining. We went for a picnic.
Although it was raining, we went for a picnic.

1 We could buy an expensive new sofa. We could just keep the old one.
2 My car is very old. Sometimes it doesn't start first time.
3 My suitcase is very heavy. I would rather use the lift.
4 Businesses are not only cutting costs. They are increasing prices.
5 I ordered a new computer over a month ago. I expect to receive it by the end of the week.
6 I told him I didn't want to book the room. He is sending us a brochure.

5 Small talk

Vocabulary: ways of talking

1a) Complete the sentences using the words or phrases in the box, putting them into the correct form.

| small talk criticise say goodbye gossip chat |
| in deep conversation moan interrupt invite |

Example: They are always _gossiping_ over a cup of coffee.

1 I called Jo for a quick _____ .
2 I hate going to parties and having to make _____ .
3 He is always _____ me when I am trying to say something.
4 I didn't want to disturb the two of them as it looked like they were _____ .
5 Why don't we _____ Michael and his wife to the party as well?
6 She is always _____ about something.
7 He _____ my management of the job.
8 Did you _____ to Jenny? She is leaving on Friday.

b) Match the following conversation extracts with the sentences above.

a) Lovely weather, isn't it? How is your wife?
b) Bye, then. Have a good time. It was lovely to see you again.
c) I was wondering if you are free on Saturday to come to a party we are organising?
d It's awful. The job is very boring, and the pay is low. And it takes me so long to get to work in the morning.
e) I really think you ought to have been able to achieve a better result than this.
f) But can I just say …
g) … and most importantly whether you feel that you are prepared to take on this major responsibility.
h) Hi, Jo, it's Nick. How are things?

Grammar: question tags

2 Match the sentences with the question tags.

1 You are coming to the party,
2 She couldn't believe her eyes,
3 You don't seriously mean that,
4 You won't be leaving early,
5 He wouldn't mind if we finished without him,
6 Let's phone and book some tickets,
7 He asked her to leave,
8 They have been working very hard,
9 She'll know where we are,
10 We can use a computer here,

a) do you?
b) shall we?
c) didn't he?
d) aren't you?
e) won't she?
f) can't we?
g) would he?
h) haven't they?
i) will you?
j) could she?

6 True love

Vocabulary: describing relationships

1 Rewrite the sentences using suitable phrases from the box. You will need to change the tenses.

| have a lot in common get together spend time apart |
| last a long time be in the public eye |
| have a happy marriage get divorced fall in love |

Example: It was love at first sight.
They fell in love immediately.

1 They became a couple at university. They …
2 They were happily married. They …
3 Their relationship lasted for years. It …
4 They shared similar interests. They …
5 Their marriage ended. They …
6 They were often in the newspapers and on TV. They …
7 They lived separately for a few years. They …

Vocabulary: phrasal verbs

2 Correct the mistakes in these sentences. Be careful – not all the sentences are wrong!

Example: After the argument, they made them up. ✗

1 They had lived apart for two years, but finally they decided to get back together.
2 We first came him across at a party.
3 He fell out with her about money.
4 'We have decided to stay together.' 'Good. I'm glad you didn't split her up.'
5 She has been ill for ages, but I think she'll get it over.
6 I get on well my parents.

3 Use the phrasal verbs in the box to fill the gaps in this diary entry. Be careful – sometimes the words are used in their literal sense.

| get back get over fall out get on (x2) come across |
| fall out take to make up (x2) split up |

What a day! It was Shirley's birthday today, so I called her in the morning. She told me she'd had an argument with Gavin. They always manage to _fall out_ about something. She said she was thinking of [1] _____ with him. Anyway, I called her in the afternoon, and apparently they had [2] _____ . He'd given her a beautiful present and everything was OK again. Typical!

    Had to get ready for the party. By the time I'd had a bath and put on my [3] _____ , it was nearly ten! I'm always late. Just as I [4] _____ the bus, I remembered I had [5] _____ Shirley's present _____ work, so I had to pop into the office to get it.

    Nice party. There was one guy called Peter I'd [6] _____ before at Gavin's house last year. We talked for about two hours. We [7] _____ very well, and at about twelve, I opened the fridge to get a drink for Peter, and a bottle of champagne [8] _____ and broke. How will I ever [9] _____ the embarrassment?! Peter soon disappeared, and I never got his phone number.

    Never mind. I enjoyed the party and I [10] _____ at about three in the morning.

7 The daddy of discipline

Vocabulary: describing behaviour

1a) Match the two halves of the phrases.

1 playing		a) naughty
2 doing		b) truant
3 doing odd		c) chores
4 getting		d) you're told
5 doing what		e) trouble
6 taking		f) jobs in the house
7 being		g) time off school
8 getting into		h) caught

b) Use the above phrases to write sentences describing the pictures.

They are ...

Grammar: obligation verbs

2 Complete the sentences using a suitable modal from the box.

> oughtn't to   need to   should   mustn't   shouldn't
> doesn't have to   must   had to

Example: Tell Jim he **doesn't have to** cook dinner tonight as we're going to get a takeaway.

1 I _____ use the computer when you have finished playing that game.
2 He _____ work so hard. He'll exhaust himself.
3 I _____ get up very early to catch the train this morning.
4 You _____ tell anyone you saw me here, or I'll lose my job.
5 They _____ leave their dog on its own all day. It gets very lonely.
6 You _____ call me when you are in town, and we can meet up for lunch.
7 He's very late. Perhaps I _____ call him.

8 That's funny

Functions: agreeing, disagreeing, giving and asking for opinions

1 *The Times* newspaper recently published lists of the top albums and the top musical artists of all time. Look at the comments made about them and correct the mistakes.

The Top 5 Albums

1 Revolver *The Beatles*
2 Sgt Pepper's Lonely Hearts Club Band *The Beatles*
3 The Beatles (White Album) *The Beatles*
4 Nevermind *Nirvana*
5 Abbey Road *The Beatles*

The Top 5 Musical Artists

1 The Beatles
2 Bob Dylan
3 Pink Floyd
4 Oasis
5 David Bowie

1 The Beatles were the top band of all time, I'm agree.
2 *Revolver* was their greatest album. I go along with that.
3 That I like about Bob Dylan is his early albums.
4 I know how you mean.
5 I love David Bowie's songs. And to you?
6 From my view, Bob Marley should be on the list.
7 What do you think to Pink Floyd?
8 I'd think that Nirvana's album isn't as good as Pink Floyd's.
9 I'm not agree with the top five albums.
10 By *The Times*, The Beatles are better than Oasis.

2 Read the following dialogues and put the words into the correct order to make appropriate responses.

1 A: Do you really think war is the only answer?
   B: solution no personally other see I
2 A: In my view, there isn't enough discipline in schools nowadays.
   B: that not sure I'm about
3 A: I think life in the city is generally more stressful than life in the country.
   B: along that go I'd with
4 A: A friend in need is a friend indeed.
   B: so you think really do ?
5 A: You remember a good teacher for ever.
   B: true view from that's of point my
6 A: I reckon most road accidents could be avoided.
   B: what see mean you I
7 A: Your schooldays are the best days of your life.
   B: you have with I'd disagree to
8 A: Personally, I don't think money brings you happiness. How about you?
   B: helps agree my but I view in it
9 A: He's a brilliant director.
   B: Absolutely! do think but of film what you his latest?

9 A perfect weekend

Vocabulary: weekend activities

1 Complete the crossword.

ACROSS

2 (and 6 across) Something you can do while sitting in a café, with your eyes open. (6, 8)
6 See 2 across
9 A short way of referring to the Internet (3, 3)
10 I've been going out too much recently. Tonight I'm just going to _____ and watch a video at home. (4, 2)
11 By Friday, my flat is always in such a mess I need to spend most of the weekend doing the _____ . (9)

DOWN

1 A type of shopping you do when you have no cash. (6)
3 I'm so unfit. I really should get some _____ . (8)
4 I'm really exhausted, but luckily tomorrow I'm not working, so I can have a long _____ . (3-2)
5 'Are you going _____ this Saturday?' 'Yes, we thought we'd try that new music bar in town.' (8)
7 'It'll be a really good party on Saturday, with lots of people you haven't seen for a while.' 'Great – it will give me a chance to _____ with everyone.' (5, 2)
8 It's strange how whenever someone gets a new house, they suddenly get really into _____ . (1, 1, 1)
10 To move around websites on the Internet. (4)

Grammar: describing future plans

2 Complete the e-mail using the verbs in the box.

| will have   are going to   aren't coming   arrives   is |
| will collect   are coming to   are planning |

Dear Jim,
Great news that you and Sal [1] _____ Edinburgh for the weekend. There [2] _____ be six of us staying in the house, so I hope it isn't too small. Your train [3] _____ at five-thirty in the morning, so we [4] _____ you from the station and drive you here. The others [5] _____ until the afternoon, so we [6] _____ to spend the morning seeing the sights and doing some shopping. The restaurant [7] _____ booked for 1.30 – and then we [8] _____ the rest of the afternoon free. Looking forward to seeing you soon.
love Jenny :-)

10 Just the job

Vocabulary: describing yourself, your skills and experience

1 <u>Underline</u> the most suitable words to complete the sentences.

Example: We are looking for a <u>*well-travelled*</u> / *innovative* / *fluent* professional with a good knowledge of the languages and customs of the Far East.

1 In order to ensure improved customer relations, the successful applicant should demonstrate excellent *managerial* / *organisational* / *communication* skills.
2 Having worked for a variety of companies, he is now a highly *dynamic* / *attentive* / *experienced* engineer.
3 A good manager is able to *motivate* / *run* / *research* team members by providing clear goals and achievable objectives.
4 The job involves managing several projects simultaneously, so good *leadership* / *IT* / *organisational* skills are an advantage.
5 My job involves *developing* / *researching* / *co-ordinating* international meetings and conferences, so I am in contact with people from all over the world.
6 His lack of clear *managerial* / *organisational* / *communication* skills meant that the workers below him decided on their own directions and priorities.
7 A group of volunteers in Dakar *ran* / *researched* / *motivated* a project to *research* / *manage* / *develop* the causes of poverty in Senegal.
8 She notices even the smallest mistakes because she has *good organisational skills* / *a good eye for detail* / *proven managerial skills*.

2 Rewrite the phrases in *italics* in the following job advertisement using suitable words or phrases from the lesson.

Example: Must *speak very good English* → Must be fluent in English.

Betta Pharmaceuticals plc

Chief Executive Officer

As a result of a complete restructuring of the organisation, we are now looking for a new CEO to take the company forward. The successful candidate will be *someone who has new ideas* and *a lot of experience in management*. He/She will *be very good at talking to people* and have the proven ability *to encourage* departments and *organise* the process of restructuring change.

The position involves *being in control of* the existing business whilst *investigating and building* a strategic plan for further expansion.

---

11 In the media

Vocabulary: the media

1 Solve the clues and find the answers in the grid.

M	Y	K	I	N	O	S	T	C	G	H	P	Z
U	N	I	Q	U	I	Z	S	H	O	W	E	R
S	A	D	O	H	N	E	A	A	N	I	R	U
I	N	O	T	U	M	O	R	T	E	T	U	B
C	O	C	O	M	E	D	Y	S	H	O	W	D
C	O	U	R	S	E	R	Q	H	V	M	I	E
H	I	M	P	S	O	A	P	O	P	E	R	A
A	X	E	L	P	A	M	S	W	I	M	E	D
N	O	N	E	O	F	A	N	Y	S	J	D	V
N	A	T	U	R	E	S	I	C	W	B	G	E
E	L	A	L	T	T	H	R	I	L	L	E	R
L	A	R	I	S	R	Y	C	O	Y	S	H	T
S	O	Y	D	H	C	A	R	T	O	O	N	S

1 Turn to these to hear the latest songs. (5, 8)
2 You can watch one of these to hear people talking about their private lives. (4, 4)
3 A serious programme to discuss issues such as politics or the environment. (11)
4 A serious play for the theatre or TV. (5)
5 These come between the programmes, when they try to sell you things like washing powder. (7)
6 Take part in one of these to answer questions and win lots of money! (4, 4)
7 Watch this if you want to have a laugh! (6, 4)
8 You can easily get addicted to this, and need to watch every episode to know what's happening. (4, 5)
9 These programmes usually have beautiful films of animals in the wild. (6)
10 These are fun for all the family, with bright colours and funny characters. (8)
11 This type of programme shows things like football matches and athletics competitions. (6)
12 This sort of film keeps you on the edge of your seat! (8)

Grammar: present perfect simple and continuous

2 Underline the correct verb form.

Example: Have you **been seeing** / **seen** the new drama series on TV? It's brilliant.

1 'You look exhausted!' 'Yes, I've **been running** / **run**.'
2 He is very pleased. He has just **won** / **been winning** a prize for his new book.
3 'You have **watched** / **been watching** TV!' 'Yes, but I've **been finishing** / **finished** my homework.'
4 I've **cooked** / **been cooking** lunch. It's nearly ready.
5 I'll be home soon – I've just **caught** / **been catching** the train.
6 'Is Mark still working in Adelaide?' 'No, he's **found** / **been finding** a new job.'

12 Ready to cook!

Vocabulary: preparing and cooking food

1 Use words from the box to complete these recipe extracts.

> grill fry boil pour simmer add chop roast serve stir melt

Example: _Grill_ the sausages under a low heat.

1 Heat the cheese until it _____ .
2 _____ the sauce over the meat.
3 _____ the carrots into small pieces.
4 _____ salt and pepper to the pasta.
5 When it is cooked, _____ hot with rice or potatoes.
6 _____ the mushrooms in a little butter.
7 Turn down the heat and allow the sauce to _____ for two minutes.
8 To _____ the chicken, place it in the oven for at least 90 minutes.
9 Bring a large pan of water to the _____ .
10 _____ the liquid regularly with a wooden spoon.

Grammar: countable/uncountable nouns and quantifiers

2 Underline the correct expression.

Example: Unfortunately, there are _few_ / _a few_ / _little_ places which are safe these days.

1 There's **a little** / **not much** / **a small number** I can do to help you, I'm afraid.
2 We had **a bit** / **a bit of** / **little** trouble with the car. That's why we are late.
3 **Every few** / **Every** / **A few** years, a new music sensation arrives.
4 **Most of** / **Most** / **Every** people believe in something.
5 Even **a small number of** / **a great deal of** / **a small amount of** sugar can be bad for your teeth.
6 I don't have **many** / **much** / **a few** free time.
7 I would like **some** / **a few** / **several** information about the museum, please.
8 I have **a large number of** / **not too many** / **a great deal of** CDs.

3 Use the phrases in the box to change the expressions in _italics_ so that they mean the opposite.

> a small number of   few   not many   a little
> a large amount of   was a great deal of   not much
> a large number of

Example: _A large number of_ women smoke in my country.
A small number of women smoke in my country.

1 There's **a lot of** beer left over from the party.
2 **Most** of us are hoping to go to university after school.
3 On the news, it said there **wasn't much** trouble on the streets.
4 Did you eat **a lot of** cake at the party?
5 **Hardly any of** the programmes on TV are worth watching.
6 **A little** money was found under the bed when he died.
7 Too **many** people are worried about the environment.

13 Contact

Vocabulary: describing gestures

1 Use the pictures to help you complete the sentences.

1 In the USA, men and women tend to _____
when they meet for the first time.
2 In Britain, if you _____ , it means 'Good luck!'
3 In Switzerland, people greet each other with a light
_____ on each _____ three times.
4 In Italy, if you _____ your _____ , it
means 'I don't know'.

Grammar: the -ing form/infinitive

2 Write the verbs in brackets in the correct form.

Example: I don't expect **to see** (see) Mike this week.

1 I can't understand how she managed _____ (leave)
her suitcase behind.
2 They have suggested _____ (go) out for a meal later.
3 She resents _____ (have) to work at weekends.
4 You can't go around _____ (shout) at people all day.
5 Sally refused _____ (let) him tell her how to run her
life.
6 He attempted _____ (open) the door without a key.
7 We try _____ (visit) my parents whenever possible.
8 I'm beginning _____ (understand) how this works.

**3 Choose the correct verb, changing the tense if
necessary.**

Example: He could **remember** remember / attempt /
expect having met her somewhere before.

1 Although she wasn't very interested, she _____
resent / pretend / refuse to enjoy herself.
2 When he arrived at the airport, he _____ **expect /
manage / continue** to find someone waiting for him.
3 The politicians _____ **choose / admit / suggest** to
ignore the warnings they had received.
4 The director of the company _____ **attempt / want /
fail** unsuccessfully to increase sales.
5 Scientists claim they have _____ **resent / manage /
continue** to find a possible cure for cancer.

14 Two cities

Vocabulary: geographical location and character

**1 Complete the sentences with the most suitable
words from the box.**

thriving cosmopolitan reputation renowned
the outskirts stunning accessible well established
vast located

Example: Florence is **located** in the heart of Tuscany.

1 Paris, _____ for its museums, is easily _____ from
London by road and rail.
2 Kraków, historically the royal capital of Poland, is now a
_____ tourist centre with many popular bars and
restaurants situated in and around the main square,
Rynek Główny.
3 Away from the centre of Manila, on _____ , you will
find a sprawling city of tin huts and cardboard houses.
4 Cape Town has earned itself a worldwide _____ for
producing a huge variety of excellent wines.
5 With thousands of immigrants arriving each year,
Vancouver is fast becoming one of the most _____
cities in Canada.
6 Mexico City is absolutely _____ (it's the world's
biggest city) and its attractions include museums,
theatres and performing-arts centres.
7 Rome, sometimes called the Eternal City, was founded
in 753BC and it is _____ as the world centre of the
Roman Catholic Church.
8 Agra in India is well known because of the beautiful Taj
Mahal. Visited by amazed tourists since the 17th
century, it is one of the world's most _____ buildings.

**2 Read the following extract from a tourist guide and
replace the words in *italics* with words or phrases from
the lesson so that the meaning remains the same.**

Example: On the **outside** of town there are ...
On the outskirts of town, there are ...

Pride of the Baltic

Why not spend the weekend in Vilnius?

■■■

This historic, [1] *lively* capital is earning a reputation
for being the most underrated in Europe. [2] *Situated*
in the south of Lithuania, Vilnius is [3] *easy to travel
to* by road, rail and air.

The [4] *beautiful* old town is [5] *well known* for its
classical and Baroque buildings. A church spire can
be seen from every street.

Start your tour in Cathedral Square, [6] *in the centre
of* the town, and stroll through Castle Street, with
its [7] *huge* variety of tourist shops and cafés, to the
[8] *old* university. At weekends, this street is
transformed into a [9] *busy* arts and craft market.

15 Round the clock

Vocabulary: describing work patterns and habits

1 Complete the sentences using phrases which include the words in brackets.

Example: She loves her job, but she never talks about anything else. She _is a complete workaholic_. (workaholic)

1 John never sleeps. He believes in working hard and playing hard. He tends to _____ . (burn)
2 She gets up at 5.30 every morning and starts planning the day. She's a real _____ . (bird)
3 He has gone to sleep because he has just finished a 24-hour shift. They make him _____ . (clock)
4 When he studies for his exams, he tends to stay up late at night and _____ . (oil)
5 As a flight attendant, on long flights she has to work from early until late. She _____ . (hours)
6 I'm very quiet in the mornings, but I wake up at night. I _____ . (owl)
7 He comes back briefly in the middle of the day because he is working _____ . (shift)

Grammar: zero, first and second conditionals

2 Fill in the gaps with an appropriate tense of the verb in brackets.

Example: I _will be_ (be) at the hotel by eleven, as long as my plane _isn't_ (be) delayed.

1 If I _____ (have) time tomorrow, I _____ (go) round and see her.
2 He _____ (get) better unless he _____ (see) a doctor.
3 If you _____ (cook), I _____ (do) the dishes.
4 I _____ (let) you watch this programme if you _____ (promise) to go straight to bed afterwards.
5 I _____ (call) him if I _____ (know) his number.
6 If I _____ (be) you, I _____ (ask) him to leave.
7 If I _____ (have) a lot on my mind, I sometimes _____ (find) it difficult to get to sleep.
8 If they _____ (call back), _____ you _____ (ask) them to leave a message?

3 Correct the mistakes in the following sentences.

Example: If I ~~go~~ to bed earlier, I wouldn't always feel so sleepy. ✗
If I went to bed earlier ...

1 When I will go to Lisbon, I will definitely send you a postcard.
2 John gets paid more if he will work overtime.
3 The world will be a better place if something was done to reduce poverty.
4 If he would call me late at night, I am usually still awake.
5 If I would pass my exam, I will be so happy.
6 I would get really bored if I would live in the country.
7 If it is my house, I will paint it all different colours.
8 If they would get back in time we can still watch the match on TV.
9 As soon as she will see the sun, she gets a tan.

16 Person to person

Vocabulary: describing people's characters

1 Find ten adjectives for describing people in the word square.

H	I	S	T	I	R	C	L	O	W	B	N	I	K	S	L
A	S	E	L	F	C	O	N	F	I	D	E	N	T	U	R
V	T	N	O	G	M	U	G	G	L	I	X	J	H	F	U
E	A	S	Y	G	O	I	N	G	R	A	T	U	O	U	O
T	W	I	S	B	O	L	L	I	N	G	A	D	U	L	L
H	A	T	P	P	D	U	S	N	A	R	C	O	G	L	H
E	T	I	Q	U	Y	S	A	G	G	A	K	W	H	Y	P
R	C	V	E	S	O	P	I	N	I	O	N	A	T	E	D
C	H	E	E	R	F	U	L	K	I	R	S	T	F	S	O
H	Z	X	R	E	A	S	S	B	D	B	N	O	U	T	T
O	M	M	B	I	G	H	E	A	D	E	D	A	L	E	X
P	U	D	D	N	S	Y	W	A	K	T	O	D	P	M	V

2 Use words from Exercise 1 to complete these sentences.

1 He's so _____ . He'll do anything to get what he wants.
2 We had dinner in a nice restaurant, but she kept talking about her ex-boyfriend. It was very _____ .
3 She doesn't get at all nervous before a show. She's very _____ .
4 He thinks he's the best at everything. He's so _____ .
5 I met his parents; they were very relaxed and _____ .
6 Be careful how you tell her the news. She can be very _____ about things like that.

Function: describing personality

3 Correct the mistakes.

Example: The thing I like ~~of~~ her is that she's very easy-going. ✗ _about_

1 Julian comes about as very shy, but once you arrive to know him, you realise he's quite self-confident.
2 She starts crying as soon as you criticise her! She's a lot sensitive.
3 The item I like about Helen is that she is always cheerful.
4 She's the class of person who can be very opinionated.
5 He always thinks about other people's feelings. There's anything very thoughtful about him.
6 He puts a lot of pressure on his workers. He is a bit pushy boss.
7 The first thing that strikes her is that she is very moody.
8 He is very fat-headed. He is always going on about how great he is.

17 Positive thinking

Vocabulary: weather idioms used for personality

1 Use these expressions to complete the sentences.

> warm   chilled out   cold   bright and breezy   dull
> hot-tempered

Example: My new boss never smiles or says hello. I think he's a very **cold** person.

1 He gets angry so quickly because he is _____ .
2 I usually feel terrible early in the morning, but my sister is always _____ as soon as she wakes up.
3 He talks about the same thing for hours. I wish he wasn't so _____ .
4 She's really _____ . Like most students at the college, she seems to relax all day.
5 They are such a _____ family – they're always very affectionate with each other.

Grammar: expressions of probability

2 Complete the horoscopes using the prompts.

Example:

Capricorn (22 Dec–20 Jan)
You are likely to (likely) meet an old friend who you haven't seen for many years.

1 **Aquarius (21 Jan–19 Feb)**
_____ (fair chance) will win something this week.

2 **Pisces (20 Feb–20 March)**
If you use your free time wisely, _____ (bound) profit. This could be a great week.

3 **Aries (21 March–20 April)**
I _____ (imagine) are feeling tired after a period of hard work. Try to put your feet up.

4 **Taurus (21 April–21 May)**
You have a busy few days ahead. _____ (definitely) have much time to enjoy yourself.

5 **Gemini (22 May–21 June)**
_____ (convinced) good times are just around the corner, and you could be right.

6 **Cancer (22 June–23 July)**
Romance is in the air! _____ (possible) meet your ideal partner this week. Be charming!

7 **Leo (24 July–23 Aug)**
You will go on a long journey this week. _____ (sure) get bored at some point.

8 **Virgo (24 Aug–23 Sept)**
This week will be colourful: flowers, song and entertainment. _____ (probably) have fun.

9 **Libra (24 Sept–23 Oct)**
Make an effort to talk to old friends this week. Some of them _____ (certain) need your help.

10 **Scorpio (24 Oct–22 Nov)**
_____ (doubtful) go out much this week, as money is tight. Take the chance to relax.

11 **Sagittarius (23 Nov–21 Dec)**
_____ (likely) will receive good news tomorrow.

18 Money talks

Vocabulary: financial terms

1 Complete the crossword.

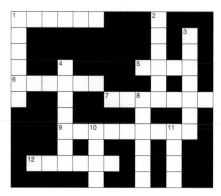

ACROSS
1 I have a huge debt with the bank that I need to _____ . (3, 3)
5 Nowadays, banks offer you a really good deal if you take out a _____ . (4)
6 It is a good time to _____ in business in the Middle East. (6)
7 I'm due to _____ some money when my uncle dies. (7)
9 I can't borrow any more money from the bank, I am already _____ . (9)
12 We'd love to buy a new car, but at the moment we really can't _____ it. (6)

DOWN
1 Initially, the dot.com businesses did well and made a good _____ . (6)
2 I need to find a part-time job to help increase my _____ . (6)
3 I pay a small amount each month into my _____ for when I retire from work. (7)
4 Their family are very _____ , so they go on expensive holidays every year. (4-3)
8 He was very _____ until he met their daughter. Now they live in a castle. (4, 2)
10 If you want to _____ a lot of money, try for a job in a bank. (4)
11 If you are paid hourly, you earn a weekly _____ . (4)

2 Complete the text using the phrases in the box.

> well-off   pensions   hard up   profit   bonuses   afford
> paying off the mortgage   paying the bills   invest

Money no object?

In a world full of credit cards, it's easy even for those of us who are **hard up** to imagine that you can ¹ _____ almost anything you want. Credit-card companies have become very good at convincing the world that money is no object. Everything from ² _____ on your house to ³ _____ like water and gas can now be done using your card. But while this might allow you to live the life of the very ⁴ _____ for a short time, in the end it is the banks who are making a ⁵ _____ . By charging interest, and using that money to ⁶ _____ in foreign business, banks are busy earning big ⁷ _____ for their staff, and offering them ⁸ _____ for when they retire.

19 Unlucky for some

Vocabulary: disaster verbs and prepositions

1 Write a sentence to describe each picture.

Example: **The cinema is burning down.**   1

2   3

4   5

Grammar: future in the past

2 <u>Underline</u> the correct alternative.

Painter Les Higgins <u>*was about to*</u> / *was about* / *going to* finish a table he had been working on when he fell off it and broke his foot. He [1] *was on the point to drive* / *was going to drive* / *was going to driving* to the hospital, but when he [2] *was about to* / *were due* / *was about* arrive, he had an accident and was fined for careless driving. He [3] *was on the point of* / *was due to* / *due to* have a peaceful recovery at home, but unfortunately his wife fell down the stairs and had to be taken to hospital, and his daughter accidentally locked herself in the toilet and had to be rescued by firefighters.

Non-swimmer Tony Turner fell into the Grand Union Canal. He [4] *was on the point of* / *was going to* / *was due to* recovering from the shock, but three days later, he fell 25 feet from the roof of his home in Paddington. He had been [5] *was about to* / *was on the point to* / *about to* catch a cat when he tripped up.

Alan Room [6] *going* / *was about to* / *was due* to have a happy and hilarious 25th birthday. He went to a comedy club with friends, but unfortunately he laughed so much that he had to be taken to hospital. When he recovered, he [7] *were about to* / *was going* / *was about to* drive home when he realised that his car had been stolen.

20 Taxi!

Vocabulary: adverbs of intensity

1 Complete the postcard with intensifiers from the box.

> absolutely   such (x2)   slightly   so (x2)   totally
> little bit   quite

Hi Sandy!
We're having an **absolutely** *amazing time here in Cuba. The people are* [1] _____ *friendly and the weather has been sunny so far. We are staying in a beautiful, old house, though it is a* [2] _____ *noisy at night. It's* [3] _____ *a pity you couldn't come. You would have loved everything about this place (even though the clubs are* [4] _____ *more expensive than we had thought). It's* [5] _____ *nice to be able to wander the streets in* [6] _____ *a historic place. I'll be* [7] _____ *sad to leave next week. Everything we had heard about it is* [8] _____ *true: great people, great music, and a fantastic atmosphere.*
Love, Tim

2 <u>Underline</u> the correct alternative.

Example: A: How was your first day at work?
           B: It was *absolutely* / *totally* / <u>*quite*</u> interesting.
              I learnt a lot.

1 A: Did you enjoy the concert?
   B: No, the music was *such* / *so* / *quite* awful that we had to leave.
2 A: Did you have a good trip?
   B: Oh, yes. The holiday was *slightly* / *absolutely* / *really* relaxing, but the journey was awful.
3 A: How do you get to school in the mornings?
   B: I come by tube. It's quite a long journey, so it's *absolutely* / *pretty* / *such* boring.
4 A: Have you heard the match results?
   B: Yes, they played *so* / *awful* / *such* terribly that they lost the game.
5 A: How was your weekend?
   B: Yesterday was *such a* / *so* / *quite* sunny day that we spent the whole time in the garden.
6 A: I'm moving to Manchester to do some research.
   B: Really? That's *rather* / *totally* / *a little bit* interesting.
7 I haven't seen my cousins for a while, so it should be a *slightly* / *fairly* / *such* enjoyable trip.
8 A: Did you enjoy the film?
   B: Yes, it was *a little bit* / *absolutely* / *quite* fantastic! The best film I've seen in years.
9 A: Did you have a nice walk?
   B: Yes, until it started to rain. We were *totally* / *so* / *little bit* wet that we had to come home.

> For more exercises, go to www.language-to-go.com   97

21 Major events

Vocabulary: news, events and disasters

1 Match the nouns with the appropriate verb phrases.

1 A volcano	a)	causes people to starve.
2 A war	b)	is signed.
3 A peace treaty	c)	make a breakthrough.
4 A bomb	d)	erupts.
5 Scientists	e)	goes off.
6 A famine	f)	breaks out.
7 Floods	g)	result in people drowning.

Grammar: passives

2 Put the verbs in brackets into the correct form.

1900s

1900 Umberto I, King of Italy, <u>was shot</u> (shoot) by an anarchist.

1903 US brothers Orville and Wilbur Wright [1] _____ (make) the first powered flight.

1908 Two-year-old Puyi [2] _____ (crown) Emperor of China.

1910s

1912 The Titanic [3] _____ (sink) after hitting an iceberg in the North Atlantic.

1914 Archduke Franz Ferdinand [4] _____ (assassinate), leading to the start of World War I.

1917 Lenin [5] _____ (seize) power in the USSR.

1920s

1920 Twenty-nine countries [6] _____ (attend) the first meeting of The League of Nations.

1921 The Chinese Communist Party [7] _____ (found).

1929 A world financial crisis [8] _____ (cause) by the Wall Street crash.

1930s

1935 The Chinese Communists' Long March, which [9] _____ (lead) by Mao Zedong, ended.

1936 The Civil War in Spain [10] _____ (begin).

1939 Britain and France [11] _____ (declare) war on Germany.

3 <u>Underline</u> the correct alternative.

1 A senior politician *was assassinated / has been assassinated / assassinated* yesterday.

2 A new planet *has discovered / has been discovered / is being discovered* by an American astronomer.

3 It is hoped that the Commanders-in-Chief of the two countries *will be agreed / will agree / will be agree* on conditions to end the fighting.

4 Yesterday, Liverpool FC *beat / were beaten / have beat* German champions, Dortmund, in the UEFA Cup Final.

5 A man who saved six drowning children *is awarded / will award / will be awarded* a special prize next month in Sydney, Australia.

6 Thousands of jobs may be lost unless new factories *are built / will be built / build*.

7 New evidence of a Stone-Age town *has found / has been founded / has been found* in England.

22 Street life

Vocabulary: street personalities

1 Unjumble the phrases and match the words to the descriptions.

1 loeeshms esnpro
2 tetsre oedvnr
3 dripaneest
4 sukrbe
5 rneftou lretle

Someone who …
a) wants to tell you about the future.
b) walks in the streets.
c) has nowhere to live.
d) wants your money in exchange for something.
e) wants you to listen and give your money.

Vocabulary: phrases with *get* and *take*

2 Write sentences with the same meaning, using either *take* or *get*.

Example: I prefer to use the bus for short journeys.
I usually <u>take the bus</u> for short journeys

Take

1 People who live in the desert tend not to be in a hurry.
People who live in the desert usually _____ .

2 I felt I hadn't made the most of my opportunities at university.
I felt I _____ the chances offered to me at university.

3 'The festival hasn't been here for years,' said John.
John said, 'The festival _____ here for years.'

4 If they laugh at me, I'll ignore them.
I _____ of them if they laugh at me.

5 If you are well prepared, it won't give you a shock.
It might _____ unless you are well prepared.

6 I expected to be healthy, so I never worried about it.
My health was something _____ .

Get

7 I hope to become familiar with my new surroundings soon.
I hope to _____ my new surroundings soon.

8 The streets here always fill up with people at about seven o'clock.
The streets _____ at about seven o'clock.

9 Is the house accessible?
Is the house easy _____ ?

10 Before injuring himself, he'd always managed to travel from place to place.
He _____ fine before the accident.

23 Gun crazy

Vocabulary: crimes and criminals

1 Complete the sentences from a report about stopping crime using the words in the box.

> kidnappers shoplifters muggers smugglers burglars
> pickpockets

1 An increase in the number of _____ has led to shopkeepers installing video cameras.
2 Tourists should be aware of _____ who operate in crowded areas like the Tube.
3 The best way to stop _____ is to leave the radio on in the house.
4 _____ tend to operate on unlit streets, late at night. They will often carry weapons such as knives, but they seldom use them.
5 _____ hide drugs in the most surprising places in order to get them into another country.
6 In some countries, it is illegal to pay money to _____ in return for the release of the people they hold.

Grammar: third and mixed conditionals

2 Underline the most suitable tenses.

1 Why didn't you tell me sooner? If you *told / had told / tell* me earlier, I *help / would help / would have helped* you.
2 All the tickets were already sold out. If I *will arrive / arrive / had arrived* there five minutes earlier, I might *be able / been able / have been able* to get us the last couple of tickets.
3 It was very dangerous. If there *was / been / had been* a car coming the other way, we *crash / had crashed / would have crashed* into it.
4 They had a fantastic holiday. They *didn't get / wouldn't have got / won't get* such a good suntan if they *hadn't been / won't been / wouldn't have been* somewhere hot and sunny.
5 Unfortunately, it rained all weekend. We *had gone / would have gone / went* on a picnic if the weather *was / wouldn't have been / hadn't been* so awful.
6 My boss is here! I *would come / wouldn't have come / wouldn't have came* if I *had known / knew / hadn't known* he was going to be here.
7 It was a disaster from the beginning. She *wouldn't have married / would never had married / would have married* him if he *hadn't told / had told / told* her about his obsession with cars.
8 The noise woke them all up. They *wouldn't realise / wouldn't have realised / didn't realise* she *had come / came / have come* home so late if she *had knocked / would have knocked / hadn't knocked* the vase over.

24 Difficult situations

Vocabulary: describing problems

1 Write sentences using the words in the boxes to describe what the problem is and what needs to be done.

> PROBLEMS
> messy dying torn mouldy doesn't work

> SOLUTIONS
> tidying mending repairing throwing away watering

Example: *My plant is dying. It needs watering.*

1   2

3   4

Functions: complaining and getting results

2 Put the words in the right order to make dialogues.

Example: A: Try to improve your handwriting, James.
   B: do best I'll my
   I'll do my best.

1 A: you possibly window the do think you could open please ?
   B: Yes, of course. It is a bit hot in here, isn't it?
2 A: It's not my fault! I did it, but then I left it on the bus.
   B: but sorry just good I'm not that's enough
3 A: I you your need I'm to to afraid talk about appearance
   B: Ah, yes. I spilled coffee on my suit. That's why I'm wearing jeans today.
4 A: Ten pounds? For a train ticket? That's far too much!
   B: there's I I'm nothing can afraid do
5 A: I think I forgot Mum's birthday last year.
   B: be you remember it it nice would if could year this
6 A: don't make but the I want to a you done fuss haven't dishes weeks six for
   B: Well, I've been busy!
7 A: Could we get a refund for this ticket? My friend can't come because he's ill.
   B: what do I'll can see we
8 A: was if bit I you lend wondering could a of me money
   B: You must be joking! You already owe me £50!
9 A: really ask to that I put out must you cigarette
   B: Oh, sorry. Is this a no-smoking area? I didn't realise.
10 A: mind the please would down you turning music ?
   B: Don't be so boring! It's a great party.

25 Under pressure

Vocabulary: expressions for annoying habits

1 Put the words in the correct order.

Example: whistle really it me when bugs people
It really bugs me when people whistle.

1 what me annoys about was I forget when it I to say
2 I keys me when it my drives can't crazy find
3 it people polite irritates aren't when me
4 find deadlines when stressful I it I to have at meet work
5 when have relief go you don't it's to Sunday to on a work
6 he'll it's to comforting that arrive ring know me when I
7 get who nerves really are on people my big-headed

Grammar: present continuous and present simple for describing change

2 Complete the sentences using suitable phrases from the box.

> is starting to come down   are more and more common
> are slowly coming to realise   is increasingly aware
> is catching on   are becoming more interested
> is still going   not following the trend
> are more often driving
> is becoming more and more difficult   the increase

Example: The number of young people using mobile phones is on **the increase**.

1 Employers _____ that worker satisfaction increases productivity.
2 Children as young as eight years old _____ in wearing designer clothes.
3 Allergies to foods and drinks _____ .
4 The government _____ that if it does not invest in public health, it will lose votes.
5 The number of traffic accidents per year _____ up.
6 The numbers of incidents involving violent crime in schools _____ .
7 Business is improving in the Asian markets. However, companies in Europe are unfortunately _____ .
8 It _____ to find local fruit and vegetables in the supermarkets.
9 The trend for taking early retirement _____ .
10 Parents _____ their children to school than letting them go on public transport.

26 At home

Vocabulary: describing houses

1 Complete this advertisement using the words in the box.

> villa   overlooks   huge   convenient   brand-new
> central heating   wooden   modern   minimalist

Mediterranean-style _villa_ in Miami. Three bedrooms. Fully equipped with ¹ _____ , dishwasher etc. The house ² _____ the sea and is ³ _____ for local amenities (excellent supermarket two minutes' walk away). This very ⁴ _____ house (built three years ago), with its ⁵ _____ garden (as big as a park!) and ⁶ _____ swimming pool (completed just two weeks ago), would be ideal for a young family. The style of the house is ⁷ _____ with just two large sofas, three chairs, a dining table and a cool ⁸ _____ floor. Rent negotiable. Call 01824 274406.

2 Find the odd one out.

Example: airy ~~overlooks~~ has central heating draughty

1 spacious tiny large warm
2 wooden modern classical elegant
3 cosy huge intimate comfortable
4 convenient minimalist isolated not far from
5 bedsit studio flat villa garden
6 basement ceiling loft third floor

3 Complete the telephone conversation with words from the lesson that mean the same as the words in brackets.

A: Hello. I'm calling about the flat I saw advertised. Could you give me some more information?
B: Of course. What would you like to know?
A: Well, I'm living in a ¹ _____ (very small) flat at the moment, so the first thing is how big is it?
B: Well, there's only one bedroom, so it's not ² _____ (very big), but it is light, so it feels ³ _____ (there is lots of room).
A: Great. And I don't like too many stairs, either. I've been living in the ⁴ _____ (roof) here.
B: No problems there. This flat is in the ⁵ _____ (underground).
A: Oh, that's good. What's it like inside?
B: Well, it's quite ⁶ _____ in style (old fashioned), with ⁷ _____ (tall rooms) and ⁸ _____ (made of wood) floors. I've just put in a new kitchen and bathroom, though, they are very ⁹ _____ (up-to-date style). There's no central heating, so it can be a little ¹⁰ _____ (cold) in winter, but there is a huge ¹¹ _____ (where you can light a fire) in the sitting room, which makes it very ¹² _____ (warm and comfortable).
A: It sounds lovely. Can I come and see it?

27 A new beginning

Vocabulary: US/UK English

1 Find the American equivalents of the following British words.

1 petrol station	4 rubbish	7 queue
2 motorway	5 tube	8 film
3 flat	6 pavement	

S	T	A	N	D	I	N	L	I	N	E
M	Y	P	H	U	B	S	K	B	I	I
S	G	A	S	S	T	A	T	I	O	N
F	A	R	H	I	E	M	O	G	S	T
R	R	T	M	D	P	O	R	A	T	A
E	B	M	T	E	S	U	B	W	A	Y
E	A	E	E	W	R	S	O	A	N	I
W	G	N	M	A	Y	L	I	Y	F	E
A	E	T	N	L	D	I	A	D	O	R
Y	H	I	M	K	O	M	O	V	I	E

Grammar: *to be/get used to*

2 Match the first parts of the sentences with the most suitable endings.

1 In Canada, we lived close to nature and we were used
2 As lazy students, we used to
3 As a child, I didn't use
4 When I took my car to France, I couldn't get
5 Artists need their own space and they aren't used to
6 Things aren't easy at work, but we'll have to

a) to like the smell of smoke.
b) used to driving on the right.
c) get used to the new manager.
d) to fishing straight from the river.
e) working with so many people.
f) get up late and do nothing all day.

3 Complete the sentences with the appropriate form of *used to*, *be used to* or *get used to*.

1 I realise it's difficult to understand the teacher, but don't worry. You'll _____ his voice.
2 Before the 20th century, women _____ vote because they weren't allowed to by law.
3 Emigrating to Australia isn't easy. There are many things you have to _____ .
4 Retiring from sport has been terrible for me. I _____ still not _____ doing no exercise at the weekend.
5 It's easier for the younger generation to use computers. They _____ working on them.
6 A few years ago, I _____ sing regularly in church, but I stopped when I joined a pop group.
7 The soldiers who fought in the desert needed to _____ the conditions quickly because there was no time for acclimatisation.
8 She doesn't mind media attention. As a politician, she _____ completely _____ it.

28 Animal magic

Grammar: relative clauses

1 Add relative pronouns to complete the questions.

Example: What's the name of the largest meat-eating animal **that** ever walked on earth?

1 What's the name of the man _____ theory of evolution was explained in his book, *On the Origin of Species*?
2 What is the country _____ has the most trees?
3 Can you explain the reason _____ vampire bats never chew their food?
4 What is the name of the man _____ studied earthquakes and whose name is now used to measure them?
5 Can you name the continent in _____ tigers are found?

Check your answers at the bottom of the page.

2 Use relative pronouns to join the sentences. If you use non-defining relative clauses, don't forget the commas.

Example: Andrew Green is a ghost hunter. His book, *Ghost hunting: a practical guide*, was published in 1973.
Andrew Green, whose book, 'Ghost hunting: a practical guide', was published in 1973, is a ghost hunter.

1 Ghost stories have been told for hundreds of years. They exist in most countries and cultures.
2 The poltergeist is a type of ghost. It does naughty things like throwing objects around a room.
3 Borley Church is the famous haunted church in England. Ghosts have been seen and strange noises have been heard.
4 The writer Martin Green was walking in Wales in 1979. He saw the ghost of a World War II plane in the sky.
5 A young couple, Carla and Thierry, and their son, Jean, had a poltergeist in their home for three years. They lived in Mulhouse, France.

3 Some of these sentences contain mistakes. Correct them.

Example: My friend Sam, who I've known ~~him~~ for years, is an actor.

1 The girl who she gave me the money disappeared.
2 The place where I live is surrounded by mountains.
3 My cousin, who is a doctor, came to visit me.
4 The day what I like best is Saturday.
5 The film, which was made in Hollywood was very popular.
6 John Grisham is a writer who's books have made him millions of dollars.
7 Shopping which is my favourite hobby is more fun in big cities.
8 The cake she made was wonderful.
9 I saw a photo of the church which my parents got married.

Answers to Exercise 1
Example: Tyrannosaurus Rex 1 Charles Darwin 2 Russia 3 They only consume blood. 4 Charles Richter 5 Asia

29 Treat yourself

Vocabulary: describing mood

1 Unjumble the words to make sentences.

Example: takes problems at off watching my baseball mind my work
Watching baseball takes my mind off my problems at work.

1 drink keep I me to coffee going
2 good always a up movie me cheers
3 feeling swimming down when me I'm calms stressed
4 make better usually flowers me feel

Grammar: *to have / get something done*

2 Rewrite the sentences using *have/get something done*.

Example: The hairdresser is cutting my sister's hair tomorrow.
My sister is having her hair cut tomorrow.

1 A man is going to paint our bathroom tomorrow.
We are …
2 A doctor took my temperature every four hours when I was in hospital.
Every four hours I …
3 The engineer is coming to repair my computer.
I'm …
4 They insured her car before she went on holiday.
She …
5 A boy delivers our newspapers every morning.
We …

3 Look at the pictures showing the day before Diane's party and the following day. Write sentences about things she has had done using the verbs in the box.

Example: *Diane has had some food delivered.*

| deliver repair clean replace move remove paint cut |

Friday

Saturday

30 Growing up

Vocabulary: ages and stages

1 Match the words with their descriptions.

1 Babies
2 Toddlers
3 Kids
4 Teenagers
5 Young adults
6 Thirty-somethings
7 Middle-aged people
8 Senior citizens

a) are (hopefully) enjoying their retirement.
b) may be in their first job and looking forward to a good career.
c) can be any age, from a few months to eighteen years.
d) aren't young or old and are often very settled in their job, home and family.
e) are at an age of discovery: they discover fashion, the opposite sex and exams.
f) cry when they are hungry.
g) have just started walking and talking.
h) sometimes feel depressed that they are no longer in their twenties!

Grammar: phrasal verbs

2 Underline the best alternatives.

We were such naughty children. I don't know how our mother *turn over / put up with / brought up / talked to* us. Our teachers said we would either [1] *turn around / grow up / find out / end up* in prison or as millionaires. One particular teacher, Mr Bowen, never let us [2] *get away with / get out of / get over / help with* anything: he used to [3] *come across us / tell us off / look after us / turn us down* for wearing the wrong uniform, for talking in class, for fighting, for anything and everything. My brother complained that he was [4] *keen on us / breaking us up / shutting us up / picking on us*, but it wasn't true. We deserved it. The only teacher we [5] *worked on / gave up on / worked with / looked up to* was Mrs Jones, who taught us music. We [6] *split up / looked forward to / kept up / turned up* her lessons because she was kind and patient, and we could make as much noise as we wanted. It's because of her that I [7] *made up / ended up / worked out / sorted out* my mind to become a teacher. And here I am, [8] *looking over / keeping up / growing up / looking after* 25 kids who are every bit as naughty as myself and my brother were.

31 Monumental mysteries

Vocabulary: measurements

1 Complete the sentences using the words in brackets in the correct form.

Example: The <u>weight</u> of the Great Pyramid of Cheops in Egypt is between 5.75 and 6.5 million tonnes. (weigh)

1 Each of the Great Pyramid's stones _____ 2.5 tonnes. (weigh)
2 The Eiffel Tower, which was the tallest building in the world from 1889 to 1930, is 300 metres _____ . (high)
3 The Pacific Ocean has an average _____ of 4,300 metres. (deep)
4 From a _____ of 40,000 kilometres, astronauts can see a number of man-made objects. (high)
5 The _____ of the Great Wall of China is 4,100 kilometres. (long)
6 _____ underground, man has discovered cave paintings which could hold clues about early civilisations. (deep)

Grammar: modals for past deduction

2 Look at the pictures and <u>underline</u> the correct alternative.

Example: The burglar *must have / can't have / might had* come through the window.

1 He *must have / can't have / might have* received bad news.

2 She *must have / couldn't had / might* committed a crime.

3 The cat *mustn't have / could have / must* eaten the dinner.

4 He *can't have / can have / might have* broken his leg.

3 Rewrite the phrases in *italics* using the words in brackets.

Example: *I'm sure it was her* that I saw because she was wearing that red coat. (must)
It must have been her ...

1 Yes, but *how do you know it wasn't* her twin sister? (might)
2 Her twin sister?! It *wasn't* her twin sister. She lives in Australia! (can't)
3 He says it *was definitely* a UFO because the lights made a strange shape in the sky. (must)
4 On the other hand, *there's a chance he was* mistaken because he had been drinking. (could)

32 Film reviews

Vocabulary: describing films

1 Complete the crossword.

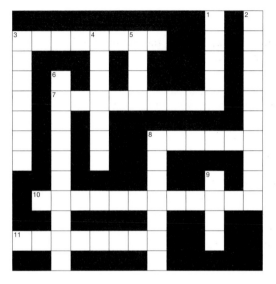

ACROSS
3 Tension in a film (8)
7 Not as good as it is supposed to be (9)
8 The written version of the film (6)
10 So stunning it might stop you from breathing! (12)
11 Place where the film is shot (8)

DOWN
1 The film was brilliant – absolutely out of this _____ (5)
2 Not the main actor but the _____ actor (10)
3 & 4 Computer-generated magic (7, 7)
5 The most famous actor in a film is usually the _____ (4)
6 The film's music (10)
8 Place where the film happens (7)
9 It was OK, if you _____ that sort of thing. (4)

Function: expressing reactions

2 Complete the dialogues by putting the words in *italics* in order.

1 A: The acting was so exaggerated.
   B: I know. It was *bit top a the over*.
2 A: I can't stand the suspense in most horror films.
   B: Me neither. *I hardly watch can to bear*.
3 A: I loved the film, but it's a shame that the cinema is so expensive.
   B: That's true, but *worth penny it every was*.
4 A: What did you think of the special effects?
   B: *out this absolutely they of were world*!
5 A: What did you think of the film?
   B: It was OK, *like you of if sort thing that*.

33 Making life easier

Vocabulary: describing machines

1 Complete the extracts from advertisements using words from the box. You may need to change the verb tense.

> indispensable help cause waste run reliable save break

Example: A guidebook is *indispensable* for tourists.

1 My computer was always _____ down, so I bought the new Supawrita.
2 Back trouble? If sitting down for long periods _____ you problems, try the new Throne Chair.
3 The most important thing about a car is that it should be _____ .
4 Are you fed up of _____ time while you wait for your kettle to boil? If so, try our Fast Boiler Kettle.
5 Automatic payment will also _____ you a lot of time.
6 Our Party Staff will _____ things _____ smoothly. Contact us for weddings, birthdays and Christmas parties.

Grammar: future perfect/continuous

2 Underline the correct form.

Example: I can't get there at eight o'clock because I'll still *be travelling* / travel / have travelled.

1 Check your e-mails tomorrow. I will *send / have sent / be sending* my article by then.
2 This time next week, I will *be relaxing / have relaxed / relax* on a tropical beach.
3 I will *work / be working / have worked* until ten o'clock tonight, so don't bother cooking for me.
4 If you don't book now, all the tickets will *have been sold / sell / be being sold* by the time you call.
5 The hostess will *wait / be waiting / have waited* for you at the airport when you arrive.
6 By the time you read this, I will *escape / have escaped / be escaped*.

3 Use verbs from the box in the future continuous or future perfect to complete the predictions.

> become work be created use live happen be made

Example: By the end of the 21st century, many workers *will have been made* redundant.

1 Many new countries _____ by the middle of the century.
2 The world's population _____ one currency some time in this century.
3 China _____ the first country with a labour force of one billion by the end of the century.
4 People _____ longer and longer.
5 By the end of 2050, a number of disasters, like earthquakes and nuclear accidents, _____ .
6 More people _____ from home than in the office.

34 In a black mood

Vocabulary: describing clothes

1 You witness a bank robbery. You see the people in the picture leaving the bank. Later you are filling out a witness report form. Complete it, using the words in the box.

> scruffy tight-fitting high heels patterned suit trainers striped baggy plain

I saw two people leaving the bank. The man looked rather *scruffy* (he hadn't shaved and wasn't very smart). He was wearing a ¹ _____ ² _____ top and he was of medium height. On his feet, he was wearing ³ _____ . The woman was wearing a ⁴ _____ (no stripes or patterns), light-grey ⁵ _____ which didn't fit (it seemed very ⁶ _____). Underneath it, she was wearing a ⁷ _____ shirt. She was trying to run, but not very successfully, because she was wearing ⁸ _____ .

Vocabulary: describing emotions

2 Unjumble the adjectives so that they match the sentences.

Example: He always needs other people's approval because he is very *insecure*. (rcsineue)

1 I was feeling _____ before my interview. (oevsnru)
2 I always feel _____ in the mornings, but after breakfast I'm a bit happier. (rmygup)
3 She's so _____ . She just can't sit still. (ertlssse)
4 Some people are always either laughing or crying, because they are _____ . (veor-mnaoieotl)
5 Sit quietly. It will help you to feel _____ and calm. (rauqtnli)
6 I feel _____ about the future: good things will happen. (itsimoitpc)
7 Artists do their best work when they are feeling _____ . (deripsni)
8 Unless you try to make friends, you'll always feel _____ . (noeyll)
9 I thought I had no chance of success, so I felt a bit _____ . (edetaitomvd)

35 Missing the mark

Vocabulary: verbs used for reporting

1 Match the verbs in the box to the sentences. You don't need to rewrite them in full.

Example: Computers will never replace books because books are beautiful objects.
argue (It can be argued that computers will never ...)

1

assure   announce   deny

a) Of course we will help you.
b) It wasn't me! I would never steal anything!
c) All trains leaving from Platform 1 will be delayed.

2

predict   point out   insist

a) I've said it once and I'll say it again: we must not give in to blackmail!
b) I think we will win the match tomorrow, easily.
c) The reason the shops are closed is that it is a bank holiday today.

3

warn   claim   confess

a) Most of the original research was actually done by me.
b) Be careful. There is a lot of ice on the road.
c) I'm guilty. I stole the money.

Grammar: constructions with reporting verbs

2 Use the words in brackets to complete the second sentences so that they mean the same as the first sentences. Write between two and five words.

Example: 'I won't tidy my room!' she said. (refuse)
She *refused to tidy* her room.

1 'Don't go to that bar, Ricky. It's dangerous,' said Ricky's father. (warn)
Ricky's father _____ to the bar.
2 'I'm getting married!' said Louise. (announce)
Louise _____ getting married.
3 'I promise you, Julie, I will return,' said Will. (assure)
Will _____ return.
4 'But I didn't eat those cakes!' said Billy. (deny)
Billy _____ the cakes.
5 'No one wants to lose their job,' said Harry. (point out)
Harry _____ no one wanted to lose their job.
6 'I invented the helicopter!' said Leo. (claim)
Leo _____ invented the helicopter.
7 'I'll be here at six o'clock.' (promise)
She _____ be there at six o'clock.
8 'I think we'll have to build more houses in future,' said the politician. (predict)
The politician _____ to build more houses in the future.

36 Now or never

Vocabulary: types of books

1 Match these books with the people who need them, or need to write them.

manual   encyclopaedia   cook book   guidebook biography   autobiography   diary   thriller volume of poetry

1 My boss is coming to dinner and he loves good food.
2 Oh, no! This stupid machine has broken down again.
3 We don't know which museums to visit.
4 I need to find out about chemicals for my science project.
5 I'd like to read all about the life of Napoleon.
6 I wish I could remember what I was doing two months ago.
7 I want everyone to know all about me. But only the good parts!
8 I need something exciting to read on the beach.
9 I want to impress her with some beautiful verse!

Grammar: participles in narratives

2 Rewrite the sentences using participles. Start each new sentence with the words in *italics* (sometimes you will need to change the verb forms).

Example: I was *feeling* hungry, and then I made myself a sandwich.
Feeling hungry, I made myself a sandwich.

1 Because I *didn't know* where to go, I asked a stranger on the street.
2 The best thing you can do to keep fit is *to run*.
3 When I *opened* the door, I realised why she loved that room.
4 Since we *have lived* here for two years, we know all the local people.
5 *I like* the actor who is playing the part of Vladimir.
6 *The interviewer* asked many questions that confused me.
7 Because I *know* John, I can tell you he would prefer to watch ballet.
8 *He saw* the girl, and she was standing by the lake.
9 It can be so dangerous *to swim* in the sea.

3 Match the two sets of sentences and link them using participles.

Example: I didn't know what to say. I kept silent.
Not knowing what to say, I kept silent.

1 He saw the open window.
2 The boy was standing close to the fire.
3 I don't come from this country.
4 I have failed to find her phone number.
5 The wind was blowing in the west.
6 I ran in the park one day.

a) It soon became a tornado.
b) I will have to visit her at home.
c) The burglar climbed into the house.
d) I bumped into an old friend.
e) He was in danger of getting burnt.
f) I don't know the customs very well.

37 The dream business

Grammar: prepositional phrases

1 Use prepositions to complete these extracts from job descriptions and advertisements.

Example: You will be expected to liaise **with** your colleagues every day.

1 We are looking for an executive director to be _____ charge _____ our network.
2 Our chain specialises _____ swimwear.
3 The company deals _____ five hundred complaints a year.
4 The successful applicant will be responsible _____ co-ordinating legal teams.
5 We take care _____ the public sector.
6 You will be expected to cope _____ a number of challenges.
7 Our company sorts _____ over ten million letters a year.
8 Applicants should concentrate _____ the skills they can offer.
9 We are concerned _____ quality above quantity.

2 Complete the second sentences using the words in brackets so that they mean the same as the first. Use between two and five words.

Example: It's my duty to check the tickets. (responsible)
I'm **responsible for checking** the tickets.

1 He gave up his job last month. (from)
   He _____ his job last month.
2 They had put some money into the company before it closed. (invested)
   They _____ the company before it closed.
3 I don't know if I'll come or not. If the weather is good, I will. If the weather is bad, I won't. (depends)
   I don't know if I'll come. _____ the weather.
4 Can you turn the music down? It's difficult for me to focus on my work. (concentrate)
   Can you turn the music down? I'm finding it hard _____ my work.
5 I've looked after dogs since I was a child. (care)
   Since I was a child, _____ dogs.
6 There are only two people in the company. (of)
   The company _____ only two people.
7 I feel ashamed about the way I behaved. (proud)
   I _____ what I did.
8 You have to communicate and maintain contact with lots of people. (liaise)
   It's important to _____ of people.
9 She didn't seem very worried about the exam. (concerned)
   She didn't seem to _____ the exam.
10 He's been the boss here for ten years. (charge)
   He _____ the company for ten years.

38 Fingers crossed

Vocabulary: body idioms

1 Find five examples of body idioms in the picture.

Example: *He's trying to make up his mind.*

Example

2 Write replies using body idioms. Don't forget to use the correct verb tenses.

Example: A: You wouldn't like him because he's always looking into other people's business.
   B: You're right. I don't like **nosy** people.

1 A: I'm taking my driving test today. Wish me luck.
   B: OK. I _____ .
2 A: Do you get on with your boss?
   B: No. We _____ .
3 A: Should I study biology or chemistry? I can't decide.
   B: You'd better _____ . Term starts next week!
4 A: Why didn't you help with the report? Too busy again?
   B: Yes. Sorry. I _____ . It's all this extra work.
5 A: How are we going to break in? There's always a guard.
   B: I'll dance around in front of him. That _____ . Then you can go in through the back door.
6 A: I've noticed that there is complete chaos in Mr Smith's class. The children are fighting and shouting all the time.
   B: Yes. Things _____ for a long time.
7 A: Were you very sad when your dog died?
   B: Yes. His death _____ . I was only seven years old.
8 A: They have been playing loud music for three hours! Is it annoying you?
   B: Yes. It _____ . Could you ask them to turn it down?
9 A: Too much television is bad for children.
   B: Yes, but _____ , it keeps them quiet.
10 A: In some cultures, schoolchildren have to memorise a lot of information.
   B: Yes. _____ is considered an important skill.

39 I wish ...

Vocabulary: describing opportunities

1 Replace the words in *italics* with a phrasal verb from the box. You may need to change the verb form.

| give up | turn down | let down | miss out on | set out |
| sign up for | put off | come off | | |

Example: My friend *managed to stop* smoking last year.
gave up

1 I wish I hadn't *refused* that job offer.
2 It was too cold, so they *postponed* the match until the following Saturday.
3 His plans didn't *become reality* because he was too lazy.
4 When he joined the army, he *lost* the opportunity to finish his education.
5 My friend *disappointed me* by not arriving on time.
6 When we *began the journey*, we were full of hope.
7 I want to *enrol on* a French course.

Grammar: *should have / if only / wish* + past perfect

2 Complete the sentences to show regret. Use the structures in brackets.

Example: I got a fine from the police because I was driving too fast.
a) I (wish / drive) **I wish I hadn't driven over the speed limit.**
b) I (should / be careful) **I should have been more careful.**

1 I paid $50 for a taxi to the airport. Later, I found out there was a bus service which cost $3.
  a) I (wish / know) about the bus
  b) I (should / take) the bus
2 I couldn't see *Romeo and Juliet* at the theatre on Broadway. All the tickets were sold out.
  a) I (wish / buy) a ticket last month
  b) I (should / book) a ticket
3 I got food poisoning because I didn't check that my food was cooked properly.
  a) (If only / check) the food
  b) I (shouldn't / eat) that chicken
4 I forgot how to speak French and English. I didn't practise enough.
  a) (If only / speak) when I had the chance
  b) I (wish / be able / practise) more
5 I'm addicted to smoking. I started when I was fifteen.
  a) I (wish / say no) when I was first offered a cigarette
  b) I (shouldn't / start) smoking
6 I used to be able to play the flute. Now I'd like to play again, but I sold my flute.
  a) (If only / sell) it
  b) I (should / keep) my flute

40 Mind your manners

Function: using social English

1 Put the words in the right order to make dialogues.

1 A: to you fancy do the going tonight theatre?
  B: but busy you the thank offer for I'm tonight
2 A: never what you'll guess
  B: What's happened?
  A: offered I've job been that
  B: Congratulations!
3 A: you kind was to look it pet my after really of
  B: was pleasure a it
4 A: but shoes me lent you lost I'm I've sorry those
  B: problem all at it's no
5 A: lovely you it to was meet
  B: again you see soon

2 Match the sentences with the appropriate responses.

Example: A: Thank you for your help.
      B: **It's no problem.**

1 Sorry. I've broken your pencil.
2 I won the general knowledge competition!
3 Did you borrow my skirt?
4 We have to go now. It's a long journey.
5 Did you say you had some news?
6 Any ideas for the weekend?
7 Would you like a cup of tea?
8 My aunt is ill.
9 It was lovely to meet you.
10 Can I get you a beer?
11 Thank you so much for looking after me.

a) Congratulations!
b) Yes. You'll never guess what. Simon's getting married!
c) How about going to a play?
d) You, too.
e) Yes. I'm afraid I spilt wine on it.
f) Don't worry about it.
g) OK. Have a good trip.
h) It was a pleasure.
i) That'd be lovely.
j) I'm sorry to hear that.
k) Thank you for the offer, but I don't drink alcohol.

3 Say which two dialogues from Exercise 2 are illustrated below.

Grammar reference

Lesson 1

Revision of tenses

- Use the **present simple** to talk about routines and habits, and for things that are true for a long time:
  *I **spend** a lot of my time in the recording studio.*
  *Music **is** the highest form of art.*

- Use the **present continuous** to talk about things that are happening at the moment …
  *What **are** you **doing**? I'**m tuning** my guitar.*

  … for temporary situations …
  *I'**m staying** with my brother until my apartment is ready.*

  … and to talk about arrangements that have been made for the future:
  *The band **is playing** at the Rock Café at seven tonight.*

- Use *going to* to talk about plans and intentions in the future:
  *I'm **going to** take up karate.*

- Use the **past simple** to talk about completed actions in the past, often with a time reference (*yesterday*, *last year* etc.):
  *He **made** his first film in 1963.*

- Use the **past continuous** to set the scene in a story …
  *The rain **was falling** and the wind **was blowing** through the trees in the dark forest.*

  … and to describe an action (finished or unfinished) which took place at a specific time in the past:
  *We **were rehearsing** yesterday afternoon.*

- Use the **past simple** and **past continuous** together in one sentence if the first action is still going on when the second action happens:
  *He **was playing** in a band when a film director first **noticed** him.*

- Use the **present perfect** to talk about your experience. It isn't important when the experiences happened:
  *He **has played** in several countries, including the USA.*

Lesson 3

Narrative tenses

- Use the **past continuous** to describe longer actions and events in the past …
  *We **were working** last Monday.*

… and to set the scene in a story:
*The sun **was shining** and a breeze **was blowing** gently across the fields.*

- Use the **past simple** and **past continuous** together in one sentence if the first action was still going on when the second action happened:
  *They **were waiting** in a queue when they **saw** each other for the first time.*

- Use the **past simple** to talk about completed actions in the past, often with a time reference (*yesterday*, *last year* etc.)
  *Sarah and Judith **grew up** on the same street.*
  *They **lived** there from 1990 to 1996.*

- Use the **past perfect simple** to talk about an action that happened before another action in the past:
  *Mary dialled the wrong number because she **had written** it down incorrectly.*

- Use the **past perfect continuous** to talk about an action that had been in progress before another action in the past:
  *I looked outside. The ground was wet. It **had been raining**.*

> Note: When telling stories, use the **past simple** to talk about main events, and all four tenses to give background information.

Lesson 4

Phrases of addition, result and contrast

- Use *also*, *as well as* and *too* to add something to a sentence:
  *A Samaritan's advice must be unprejudiced **as well as** confidential.*
  *The Samaritans work long shifts, **too**.*

> Note: *Too* is the only one that can go at the end of a sentence.

- Use *because of this*, *as a result* and *therefore* to talk about results:
  ***Because of this**, the Samaritans couldn't give their own opinions.*

- Use *nevertheless*, *however*, *on the other hand* and *although* to make a contrast:
  ***Although** the Samaritans work long hours, they aren't paid.*

> Note: *Although* never goes at the end of a sentence.

Lesson 5

Question tags

- Use questions tags to check information or to ask someone to agree with you:
  The exhibition is on until next week, **isn't it?**
  The film was brilliant, **wasn't it?**

  The difference between checking and asking for agreement is conveyed by intonation (see below).

- To form question tags:

  If the first part of the sentence is positive, the question tag is negative:
  It**'s** a beautiful painting, **isn't it?**

  If the first part of the sentence is negative, the question tag is positive:
  The exhibition **doesn't close** at lunchtime, **does it?**

  If the main part of the sentence contains an auxiliary verb or the verb **be**, repeat it in the question tag:
  He **hasn't** read the book yet, **has he?**
  We **don't** have any eggs, **do we?**
  You **can** ride a bike, **can't you?**
  He**'d** like a new job, **wouldn't he?**
  We**'re** ready to go, **aren't we?**

  If the main part of the sentence does not contain an auxiliary or the verb **be**, use **do** in the question tag:
  Kate made all the food herself, **didn't she?**
  You finish work at five, **don't you?**

- After a positive imperative in the main part of the sentence, use **will**, **would**, **can** or **could** in the question tag:
  Pass me the dictionary, **will you?**
  Help me carry these cases, **would you?**

  After a negative imperative, use **will you**:
  Don't forget to post the letter, **will you?**

  After **let's**, use **shall we**:
  Let's eat out tonight, **shall we?**

> **Note:** When the question tag is a real question and you are not sure of the answer, use rising intonation:
>
> The museum is open today, isn't it? ↗
>
> When you are sure of the answer and are just asking for agreement, use falling intonation:
>
> The shops are very crowded today, aren't they? ↘

Lesson 6

Phrasal verbs

- The particle following the verb can be a preposition or an adverb:
  come across   split up

- Transitive phrasal verbs take a noun or object pronoun:
  She **took to him** immediately.

  Where the particle is an adverb, the object precedes it:
  He **told Phil off** for not doing his homework.

  Where the particle is a preposition, the object follows it:
  She **came across it** in an old bookshop.

- Intransitive phrasal verbs have no object:
  They had an argument and **fell out**.

- Some phrasal verbs have three parts: verb + adverb + preposition:
  Mary **split up with** Paul after five years.
  I'm trying to **cut down on** coffee.
  Mary and Paul have **got back together**.

- Some intransitive verbs can be used transitively with the addition of a preposition:
  They **got on** well.   She **got on with** him.

Lesson 7

Obligation verbs

- Use **should** or **ought to** to say what you think is the right thing to do (to give advice or suggestions):
  You **should** take your marriage seriously.
  You **ought to** spend more time together.

- Use **supposed to** to give advice based on a rule or prior arrangement:
  You're **not supposed to** chew gum in class.
  You're **supposed to** be there at ten.

- Use **supposed to** to talk about obligations that come from other people:
  I'm **supposed to** be home by ten every night.
  I'm **not supposed to** stay out late.

- Use **mustn't** to talk about prohibition:
  You **mustn't** talk to strangers.

- Use **need to** and **have to** to talk about obligations:
  I **need to** get up early tomorrow. I've got a lot of work to do.
  I **have to** stay in tonight and look after my younger brother.

- Use *don't have to* and *needn't* to say that something isn't necessary:
  I *don't have to* wear a uniform.
  You *needn't* wear a jacket to the party. It's very informal.

Lesson 8

Agreeing, disagreeing, giving and asking for opinions

Use *I would* (*I'd*) to soften the opinion you are giving:

A: *I think comedy is the best medicine there is.*
B: *I'd have to disagree with you.*

A: *Comedy is a funny way of being serious.*
B: *Yes, I'd go along with that.*

Lesson 9

Tenses for describing future plans

- Use *going to* to talk about intentions …
  I'm going to have a party in the summer.

  … and predictions based on present evidence:
  It's going to be a beautiful day – look at that blue sky!

- Use the **present continuous** to talk about arrangements you've made for the future:
  I'm seeing John on Monday.

- Use the **present simple** to talk about fixed future events, especially with programmes and timetables:
  The plane lands at 10.45.

- Use *will* to talk about spontaneous decisions:
  A: *I'm having lunch with Frank today.*
  B: *Great! I'll come too.*

Lesson 11

Present perfect: simple/continuous

- Use both the **present perfect simple** and the **present perfect continuous** to talk about recent actions and situations that have a result in the present.

  Use the **present perfect simple** when you focus on the result of a completed activity:
  I've worked on several TV programmes.
  (so I have some experience of TV programming now)

  Use the **present perfect continuous** when you focus on the activity. The activity may or may not be completed:
  I'm tired – I've been working on that project again.

- Use both the **present perfect simple** and the **present perfect continuous** to talk about actions and situations that started in the past and continue up to the present. They may be unfinished:
  I've been working on that project for six months.
  I've worked in TV for five years.

> Note: There is often little difference in meaning in these cases.

Lesson 12

Countable/uncountable nouns and quantifiers

- Use these quantifying expressions with **countable nouns**: *a few, several, each, a small number of, not too many, every few, not a large number of.*
  Use *a few onions, several spoons* of oil …

- Use these quantifying expressions with **uncountable nouns**: *a little, a small amount of, a bit of, not too much, a great deal of.*
  Use *a little oil*, and *a small amount of flour* …

- Use these expressions with both **countable** and **uncountable nouns**: *some, any, most of, all, almost all.*
  Use *almost all the oil* and *all the potatoes. Mix in some onions and some salt* …

> Note: Use *few* (with countable nouns) and *little* (with uncountable nouns) to emphasise a lack of something. *A few* and *a little* mean a small quantity, but have a more positive tone:
> *There are few places where you can buy good pasta round here.*
> (There aren't many shops – we need more.)
> *There are a few places where you can buy good pasta round here.*
> (There are some shops – we have a choice.)

Lesson 13

The -ing form/infinitive

- Use the *-ing* form or a noun after a preposition:
  I'm sick of pretending to be friendly.
  I'm fed up with my work.
  I'm bored of him talking about his problems the whole time.

- Use the *-ing* form or a noun after these verbs: *like, love, enjoy, hate, don't mind, can't stand, avoid, admit, resent.*
  The English avoid touching each other if at all possible.
  I enjoy aerobics.

- You can use an infinitive instead of the *-ing* form after *like*, *love* and *hate* with little change in meaning:
  I like to swim/like swimming when I get the chance.
  We love to see/love seeing you – you know that!
  I hate to say/hate saying this, but that colour doesn't really suit you.

- Use the infinitive with *to* after these verbs: *want*, *decide*, *need*, *learn*, *promise*, *choose*, *refuse*, *manage*, *attempt*, *would like/love/hate*:
  The boxer refused to shake hands with his opponent.

- Use the infinitive without *to* after modal verbs (*can*, *will*, *should*, *must* etc.)
  I must go out.

- You can use the *-ing* form or the infinitive after *continue* with no change of meaning:
  He continued clapping/continued to clap long after everyone else had stopped.

- You can use the *-ing* form or the infinitive after these verbs, but there is a change in meaning: *remember*, *try*, *go on*, *forget*, *stop*:
  I remember shaking hands with him. (I shook hands. Now I remember it.)
  I remembered to shake hands with him. (I saw him, I remembered what to do, so I shook hands.)

  He stopped hugging me. (He was hugging me and then he stopped.)
  He stopped to hug me. (He stopped what he was doing so that he could hug me.)

Lesson 15

Zero, first and second conditionals

- **Zero conditional**
  Form: *If* + present simple + present simple
  Use the zero conditional to talk about things that are usually true:
  If you have an important decision to make, it's often difficult.

- **First conditional**
  Form: *If* + present simple + *will*
  Use the first conditional to talk about things that may or may not happen in the future or that are a probable situation in the future:
  If the trend continues, this figure will double in the next ten years.

- **Second conditional**
  Form: *If* + past simple + *would/could*
  Use the second conditional to talk about less likely or hypothetical situations:

If you had more money, you could buy a house in LA.
If you bought a house in Las Vegas, you'd regret it.

Notes

- With *I*, *he*, *she* and *it*, you can use *were* or *was*:
  If I were rich … If it weren't raining …

- In conditional sentences, the *if* clause often comes first but it can come second:
  If I were younger, I'd be happier.
  I'd be happier if I were younger.
  When the *if* clause comes first, put a comma after it. You don't need a comma when it comes second.

- You can use *provided that* and *as long as* instead of *if*, but note that these are more formal:
  Provided that you enjoy working at night, this isn't a bad job.
  As long as you enjoy working at night, this isn't a bad job.

- *Unless* means *if not*:
  Don't take the job unless you enjoy working at night.
  (Don't take the job if you don't like working at night.)

Lesson 16

Describing personality

Use the present continuous + *always* to describe people's habits:
I love Tony. He's always buying me flowers and making sure I'm happy.
Patricia is very annoying. She's always complaining about something.

Lesson 17

Expressions of probability

- Use expressions like these to talk about probability in the future:
  It's bound to …
  It's quite possible that …
  You'll probably …
  I'm fairly convinced that …

  It's bound to rain tomorrow. (I'm sure that's what will happen.)
  It's quite possible that John will ring tonight. (I think this is likely.)

- Form

is/are + phrase + *to*	*They're bound to come.*
It's + adjective (+ *that*) + *will*	*It's unlikely that he'll ring.*
phrase (+ *that*) … *will*	*We're pretty convinced that it'll rain.*
will + adverb	*She'll certainly visit us next month.*
adverb + *won't*	*They definitely won't want to leave so early.*

Lesson 19

Future in the past

- Use *was/were going to* to talk about intentions that didn't happen:
  *I **was going to ring** you yesterday, but I ran out of time.* (I intended to ring you, but I didn't ring you.)
  *I **was going to come** and pick you up tomorrow, but I'm afraid I can't.* (I had a plan to pick you up tomorrow, but I won't pick you up tomorrow.)

- Use *was/were about to* and *was/were on the point of* to talk about intentions that you thought would happen very soon, but didn't happen:
  *I **was about to start** cooking when he arrived.* (I was just going to start cooking, but he arrived so I didn't.)
  *We **were on the point of driving off** when we realised the tyre was flat.* (We were just going to drive off, but we realised we had a flat tyre, so we didn't.)

- Use *was/were due to* to talk about an arranged plan which didn't happen:
  *I **was due to go** to the dentist last Wednesday, but I had to cancel.* (I had an appointment with the dentist, but I didn't go.)

Lesson 20

So/such

- Use *so* and *such* for emphasis:

so + adjective	*He's **so clever**.* *That dog is **so naughty**.*
such (+ *a/an*) + adjective + noun	*He's **such a nice man**.* *The Wilsons are **such nice people**.* *They have **such noisy** children.*

- Use *so ... that* and *such ... that* to give a reason:
  *The book was **so** interesting **that** I couldn't put it down.*
  *We had **such** a nice time in Greece **that** we're going to go back next year.*

> **Note:** When *such* (*a/an*) is used after a negative, it often has the effect of softening rather than emphasising:
> *That's **not such a good idea**.*

Lesson 21

Passives

- To form the passive, use *be* in the correct tense + past participle:
  *The world high-jump record **has been broken**.*

- Use the passive when you are not interested in who does the action, or it isn't important who does it:
  *The Berlin Wall **was built** in 1961.* (It isn't important who built it.)

- The passive can also be used to shift the emphasis to the end of a sentence:
  *The crops **have been destroyed**.*

- If you want to say who does the action, use *by* + person/thing:
  *The telephone was invented **by Alexander Graham Bell**.*
  *The Earth will be ruined **by pollution**.*

Lesson 23

Third and mixed conditionals

- **Third conditional**
  Form: *If* + past perfect + *would/could/might have* + past participle

  Use the third conditional to talk about how things might have been different in the past (note the slight changes in meaning):

  *If she'**d arrived** earlier, I'**d have seen** her.* (I definitely would have seen her, but she didn't arrive earlier, so I didn't see her.)
  *If she'**d arrived** earlier, I **might have seen** her.* (Perhaps I'd have seen her, but I'm not sure.)
  *If she'**d arrived** earlier, I **could have seen** her.* (It would have been possible for me to see her.)

- **Mixed conditional**
  It's possible to use a different time reference in the conditional clause:
  *If I **had stolen** the jewels, I'**d be** in prison today.*
    in the past   in the present
  (But I didn't steal the jewels, and I'm not in prison.)

> **Note:** The *if* clause often comes first, but it can come second:
> *If I had stolen the jewels, I'd be in prison today.*
> *I'd be in prison today if I'd stolen the jewels.*
>
> When the *if* clause comes first, put a comma after it. You don't need a comma when it comes second.

Lesson 24

Complaining and getting results

We often use **conditionals** to complain about things and *will* to offer help.
*It **would** help if you did the washing up sometimes.*
*I wonder if you **could** do the shopping from time to time.*

I'll see what I can do.
I'll do my best to help you.

Lesson 25

Present continuous for describing change

Use the **present continuous** to talk about changing or developing situations:
*Employers **are beginning** to use laughter therapy to increase workers' productivity.*
*The business world **is becoming** increasingly aware of the problems of stress.*

Lesson 27

To be/get used to

- Use **used to** + infinitive for repeated actions in the past that don't happen now:
  *I **used to** take the tram. (But now I don't.)*
  *I **didn't use** to take much exercise. (But now I do.)*
  ***Did** you **use** to drive to work?*

> Note: The negative and interrogative forms have *use*, not *used*.

- Use **used to** + infinitive to talk about past states:
  *Billy **used to** love football. (But now he doesn't.)*

- Use **be used to** + noun or **-ing** form to say that you are familiar with something:
  *Martine **is used to** British food now. (She's been in England a long time.)*
  *The children **are used to travelling** by bus. (They do it often.)*
  *I'm **not used to staying** up so late. (This is unfamiliar. I don't usually stay up late.)*

- Use **get used to** to describe the process of becoming used to something:
  *I hate getting up so early, but I'm **getting used to** it.*

Lesson 28

Relative clauses

- Use defining and non-defining clauses to add information to a sentence.

- Use defining relative clauses to give *essential* information about the preceding noun or pronoun in the sentence. The clause *defines* the person, thing or place you are talking about.
  *A shark is an animal **that lives in the sea**.*

- Use a relative pronoun (**who, which, that, where, when**) to introduce defining relative clauses. You don't need a relative pronoun when you are defining the object of a sentence:
  *Blood is the smell (**that**) sharks like the most.*

- Use non-defining relative clauses to give *extra*, non-essential information about the subject of the sentence:
  *The shark, **which can detect a swimmer from far away**, has electric sensors in its body.*

- Use **who, which** and **where** in non-defining relative clauses.
  *My sister, **who** is a lifeguard, was once bitten by a shark.*
  *The Great Barrier Reef, **where** you can find several species of shark, is extremely beautiful.*

- Non-defining relative clauses may also come at the end of a sentence:
  *The swimmer saw the shark approaching, **which was extremely frightening**.*

> Note: Non-defining relative clauses are separated from the rest of the sentence by commas at the beginning (and end) of the clause. Do not use commas in defining relative clauses. Sometimes the commas are the only thing that tell you whether a clause is defining or non-defining, and can change the meaning:
> *I have a friend who lives in Ireland. (I have lots of friends, one of whom lives in Ireland.)*
> *I have a friend, who lives in Ireland. (I have one friend, and that friend lives in Ireland.)*

Lesson 29

To have/get something done

- Use the causative to say that somebody does something for you:
  *I **have my hair cut** once a month. (Somebody cuts it for me. I don't cut it.)*
  *We **get the papers delivered**. (Somebody delivers the papers to our house for us.)*

- Form:
  have/get + object + past participle
  *I **get my car serviced** once a year.*

- Use the causative to say that something happens to you. Often these are unpleasant things:
  *I **had my wallet stolen**.*

> Note: We do not usually use **get** in these situations. **Get** implies that the speaker is happy for the action to take place.

- Use the causative in the imperative form to give an order:
  Get your hair cut!

> Note: It is more usual to use **get** than **have** in the imperative.

Lesson 31

Modals for past deduction

- Use past modal verbs (*must have*, *can't have*, *might have* etc.) to make deductions about the past based on facts.

- Use *must have* + past participle to say that you're sure that something was true:
  *The Mayans **must have been** experts in mathematics.*

- Use *can't have* + past participle to say that you're sure something was impossible:
  *They **can't have used** wheeled transport to move the stones.*

- Use *might/may/could* + *have* + past participle to say that you think something was possible:
  *They **could have floated** the stones across the river.*

- You can also use *must*, *can't*, *might*, *may*, *could* to make deductions about the present:
  *That **must be** John at the door.*
  *It **might be** Ann.*
  *It **could be** Sue.*

> Note: Deductions made about the present are based on hypotheses; deductions made about the past are based on facts.

Lesson 32

Expressing reactions

- Use intensifiers (*rather*, *quite*, *fairly*, *very*, *really* etc.) with adjectives to strengthen or weaken what you are saying.

- Some intensifiers weaken the adjective:
  *The food is **fairly** good.* (It's OK – not very special.)
  *This report is **slightly** worrying.* (I'm worried about it, but not too much.)

- Other intensifiers strengthen the adjective:
  *The food is **really** good.* (It's good. I like it a lot.)
  *This is a **particularly** interesting problem.* (It's very interesting.)

- *Quite* has two meanings:
  1) *quite* + gradable adjective:
  *The film is **quite** entertaining.* (It's all right.)
  2) *quite* + non-gradable adjective
  *The film is **quite** brilliant!* (It's completely brilliant.)

> Note: Americans only use *quite* in the first of these two ways.

- Use *absolutely* and *totally* only with very strong adjectives:
  *Patrick is **absolutely amazing**.*   not   ~~Patrick is absolutely good.~~

  *He's **totally brilliant**.*   not   ~~He's totally nice.~~

Lesson 33

Future perfect and future continuous

- Use the **future perfect** to describe an action or state that will be finished before or at a time in the future.
  *By the end of the century, inventors **will have designed** a voice box that translates automatically.*
  *By 2015, **I will have learnt** three new languages.*

  Form: *will* + *have* + past participle

- Use the **future continuous** to describe an ongoing activity that will be in progress at a time in the future.
  *In the near future, everyone **will be speaking** the same language.*
  *In the next century, we **will all be living** in spaceships.*

  Form: *will* + *be* + *-ing* form

- Note the difference between the **future simple** and the **future continuous**:
  *The children **will laugh** when they see the clown.* (The clown will arrive and the children will laugh.)
  *The children **will be laughing** when the clown arrives.* (The children will start laughing before the clown arrives.)

Lesson 35

Constructions with reporting verbs

- There are several reporting verb and patterns you can use in reported speech. Here are some common ones:

  - verb (+ *that*)
    accept, admit, advise, agree, announce, believe, claim, complain, confess, decide, deny, expect, explain, insist, know, predict, promise, repeat, reply, say, suggest
    *He **agreed (that)** I had lent him the book.*

  - verb + object (+ *that*)
    assure, inform, reassure, remind, tell, warn
    *She **assured him (that)** she would be there.*

  - verb + *to* + infinitive
    agree, claim, demand, guarantee, offer, propose, refuse, threaten
    *They **offered to help** him with the project.*

  - verb + *to* + *-ing* form
    admit, confess
    *He **confessed to being** at the murder scene.*

Note: Some verbs, such as *admit*, *claim* and *confess*, can be used in more than one pattern:
*He confessed **that** he had stolen the money.*
*He confessed **to** stealing the money.*

- When a statement is still relevant or important now, the verb in the reported speech doesn't change.
  *'I**'m** going to resign from my job.'*
  *He said he**'s** going to resign from his job.* (He still intends to resign.)

  However, if the statement is no longer relevant or important, the tense changes as normal.
  *He said he **was** going to resign from his job.* (And he either did or didn't.)

Note: The reporting verb can also be used in the present tense if the statement was made very recently or refers to an ongoing situation:
*He **says** he's going to resign from his job.*

Lesson 36

Participles in narratives

- **Present participles** can be used to reduce clauses.

- Use present participles:

  - when two actions happen at the same time:
    ***Peering** into the darkness, he heard a scream.* (When he peered ...)

  - to give the reason for an action:
    ***Realising** he couldn't escape, Henry sat and waited.* (When he realised ...)

  - as adjectives:
    *With each **passing** minute, he felt more and more nervous.* (With each minute that passed ...)

  - as nouns:
    ***Working** too hard can be very bad for you.* (If you work too hard ...)

  - after verbs of sensation (*see*, *feel*, *hear* etc.):
    *He felt someone **watching** him.* (He felt that someone was watching him.)

Note: Present participles are often used as a literary device in narratives (novels etc.).

Lesson 37

Prepositional phrases

Many verbs are followed by **prepositions**. Sometimes the choice of preposition depends on the meaning:

*Tim agreed **to** Pam's suggestion.*
*Jane agreed **with** me that the litter in the town was a problem.*

*Don't worry – I'll deal **with** the money, you look after the passports.*
*The firm deals **in** second-hand cars.*

Note: Like phrasal verbs with prepositions, verbs + prepositions can't be separated by the object:
~~The firm deals second-hand cars in.~~

Lesson 39

Should have/ if only/ wish + past perfect

- Use *I should/shouldn't + have* + past participle to say that you regret doing or not doing something:
  *I **should have called** him.* (but I didn't)
  *I **shouldn't have lied** to you.* (but I did)

- You can also use *I wish I had/hadn't* + past participle and *If only I had/hadn't* + past participle:
  *I wish I **had** asked him for his autograph!* (but I didn't)
  *If only I **hadn't** been so shy!* (but I was)

Note: These expressions are slightly stronger than *should/shouldn't have* and express more regret about the situation.

- You can blame someone for doing or not doing something by using *You should/shouldn't + have +* past participle:
  *You **should have asked** me first.*
  *You **shouldn't have said** that.*

Lesson 40

Using social English

Some everyday expressions are followed by an *-ing* form, others by the infinitive. Here are some common ones:

+ *-ing* FORM
*How about **going** out tonight?*
*Do you fancy **watching** this film?*
*Thanks so much for **taking** me to the station.*

+ INFINITIVE
*I'd love **to go** out.*
*It would be lovely **to go** for a walk.*
*I'm sorry **to disappoint** you.*
*It was kind of you **to visit**.*
*It was lovely **to see** you.*

Recording scripts

Lesson 1 Getting ahead

Exercise 3

I = Interviewer C = Chris

I: Chris, can you tell us a little bit about your attitudes towards music and how you got into it?

C: I believe music is the highest form of art and the purest form of expression and I've loved it for as long as I can remember. I think I first really got into it when I was listening to records in my bedroom while I was still at school.

I: When did you realise you were going to do it professionally?

C: I didn't know I could do it for a living until I realised people enjoyed listening to the music me and my friends were making. That you could reach people with music. And it was better than a real job.

I: Right. Have there been any special memories or moments?

C: Lots. It was exciting playing with Lloyd Cole and Richard Butler of the group The Psychedelic Furs, who were heroes of mine when I was younger.

I: And what else has the music business given you?

C: Travel. I've been able to see the world. I've been lucky enough to have toured Japan, Europe, the USA, Central America. And the opportunity to meet people.

I: And what are you working on at the moment?

C: At the moment, I'm working on a project with some musicians in New York. We're doing two recordings at the end of the month and hopefully we're going to start touring after that.

I: Right. And what about the future? What are your ambitions?

C: Meeting and playing with as many musicians as possible. Also playing different styles. You should try and broaden your horizons as much as possible. Music is an evolving thing and you have to keep evolving with it.

Lesson 2 Modern survival

Exercise 3

I = Interviewer C = Dr Cave

I: So, Dr Cave, why is it that some countries have higher life expectancies than others?

C: Well, obviously there are lots of important factors here. The physical conditions in the country, the climate, war, of course, and famine. Interestingly though, probably the most important factor in determining life expectancy is, in fact, our genetic history.

I: Really? Our genes?

C: Well, yes, it depends on how healthy our parents are, and even our grandparents before that. And not just their genes, but their lifestyles, too.

I: Genetics. So if we want to live longer, we really need to choose our parents carefully? Isn't there anything we can do ourselves?

C: Yes, of course, there is a lot we can do. Men, funnily enough, one of the things they can do is to get married, and preferably to a younger woman. It seems that late marriage and particularly children in later life is one of the things that keeps husbands and fathers young and in good shape. Women, however, have a greater chance of living longer if they avoid marriage.

I: And what about lifestyle? Is there such a thing as a healthy lifestyle to help us live longer?

C: Yes, living in the country, for example, as opposed to the city. That makes a difference. Diet, eating carefully, having a healthy balanced diet is important, not too many saturated fats.

I: So we do need to watch our weight?

C: Well, you need to be careful not to overdo it. Putting on a lot of weight in a short space of time, or losing it quickly for that matter, is very unhealthy. Just keep an eye on things and cut down on excesses – too much chocolate and fatty or fried foods.

I: I see, and what about alcohol?

C: Well, a little wine is OK, but for a really healthy lifestyle you would have to give up alcohol, smoking and all that kind of thing.

I: That doesn't sound much fun.

C: No, and it needs to be fun. Life must be entertaining, and this is something people often forget about. It's been shown that depressed people tend to die younger. We need life to be filled with interests and physical activities. I mean, you don't necessarily need to go jogging every day or work out in the gym to be in good shape. A brisk walk would do the job, twenty-five minutes. Walk to work, for example, rather than catch the bus. And some mental activity, too, a bit of intellectual exercise, a crossword or puzzle, doing your tax accounts maybe – something to keep the brain fit.

I: And how about stress? How does that affect us?

C: To be avoided, really. If you do lead a very busy life, you need to find time to relieve the stress. Exercise does that, it releases the endorphines in the brain and helps you relax. Massage is very good, too.

I: Lovely. Any other tips?

C: Water. Drink as much as possible. And sleep – about eight hours' sleep, no longer, but have a good rest after lunch.

Lesson 3 Coincidences

Exercise 6

Sarah Jones and Judith Thomson, from England, grew up on the same street and became best friends. Judith was Sarah's bridesmaid in 1947. Then Sarah emigrated to the USA and they lost touch. Fifty-three years later, they bumped into each other while they were waiting in a queue at a petrol station in Nevada, USA.

Lesson 4 Friends

Exercise 5

I = Interviewer C = Chris

I: According to a survey published in today's Metro newspaper, we have fewer friends today than ever before. The average city-dwelling thirty- or forty-something has about three close friends, as well as a few 'semi-detached' ones. Joining us now to discuss this phenomenon is Chris Johnson, a counsellor. Chris, does this surprise you?

C: It doesn't really surprise me. I think the thing is people don't seem to have the time, or don't think they have the time, to see their friends, and therefore we don't have as many as our grandparents' generation. And that, according to this report, is the big difference between friendships now and friendships twenty or thirty years ago.

I: We're busy and, as a result, we don't socialise?

C: No, I think we do. However, we also apply the same principles to friendship as we do to anything else in life. Why sit around the kitchen table having coffee with your best mate when you could be finishing a report for work or in the gym getting fit?

I: On the other hand, why bother going to the gym when you could be spending time with friends?

C: Absolutely. I agree. Most of the calls I get are from people who have great problems and are suffering from this lack of friendship too. Because of this, they don't have anyone to turn to when the problems get on top of them.

I: Although you'd have thought that, with modern-day means of communication particularly, it's easier to keep in touch with people.

C: Yes, but nevertheless, something like the Internet doesn't really bond people, does it? I mean, whatever gets written or communicated, a computer screen is no substitute for a friend in the flesh.

Lesson 5 Small talk

Exercise 5

Example
A: The weather's been lovely, hasn't it? What did you get up to over the weekend?

Conversation 1
B: We had terrible trouble getting here.
C: Really? It doesn't usually take long, does it?
B: No, but first we were delayed, and then the train was cancelled.

Conversation 2
D: It was a fantastic film, wasn't it?
E: Yes. Brilliant.
F: Really? I haven't seen it yet.
E: Oh, you must. Let's go together, shall we?

Conversation 3
G: I mean, you can't seriously call that art, can you? It's so ugly, isn't it? You're not the artist, are you?
H: Actually it's a fake, but you won't tell anyone, will you?

Conversation 4

I: Times have changed, haven't they? Life was very different then. When I was a boy we used to …
J: Excuse me a moment.

Conversation 5

K: See you at the exhibition on Sunday. You will be there, won't you?
L: I can't wait.

Exercise 10

Example: He's gorgeous, isn't he?
        Yes, he is. I …

1 It's been fantastic weather, hasn't it?
  Yes, it has. Yesterday I …
2 It was an awful journey, wasn't it?
  Yes, it was. I couldn't believe how …
3 She made all this food herself, didn't she?
  Yes, she did. And it's so delicious I …
4 There isn't any more wine, is there?
  Yes, there is. Would you like …
5 You don't happen to know where the toilet is, do you?
  Yes, I do. It's over …
6 She could have rung to say she wasn't coming, couldn't she?
  Yes, she could. It's not like her to …
7 You will stay for dinner, won't you?
  No, we can't. We've got friends …
8 They can't have forgotten, can they?
  No, they can't. We spoke to them …
9 You work in computers, don't you?
  Yes, I do. I design websites for a company …

Lesson 6 True love

Exercise 7

Marilyn Monroe, one of the cinema's most famous faces, married her first husband when she was sixteen, but they didn't get on and four years later, they got divorced. In 1954, she married the baseball star, Joe DiMaggio. They fell out frequently, though, and separated. The following year, she came across Arthur Miller while she was in New York. After a five-year marriage, they, too, split up. In 1962, she made up with DiMaggio and they got back together. They were planning to get married again, but she died after taking an overdose of sleeping pills. Monroe entertained millions of people but never found lasting happiness. Some say she never got over the problems of her lonely childhood.

Exercise 8

They didn't get on.
They fell out frequently.
She came across Arthur Miller in New York.
They, too, split up.
She made up with DiMaggio.
They got back together.
She never got over the problems of her childhood.

Lesson 7 The daddy of discipline

Exercise 8

Example: I really ought to revise for my exams next week.

1 We don't have to wear uniforms at school.
2 You ought to help your mother by washing the dishes.
3 She shouldn't worry about us. We'll be fine.
4 You should ask him before you take the car.
5 I shouldn't eat so much junk food.
6 You mustn't speak to any strangers in the street.

Lesson 8 That's funny

Exercise 3

I = Interviewer

A: What makes me laugh? I suppose if someone tells a good joke. I quite like verbal humour, but the timing has to be just right.
I: I know what you mean. And what about visual humour? What do you think of clowns and that sort of thing?
A: I'm not really into physical humour and clowns. They just look stupid to me. But when I was younger, I loved cartoons, things like Tom and Jerry, and I still find them quite funny.
I: Yeah, I'd have to agree with you.
B: You British people tend to go in for irony. But from my point of view, a man slipping on a banana skin is still the funniest thing ever.
I: Oh, I'm not sure about that. It's too obvious for me.
B: Really? I reckon that type of humour is truly international and that's why people like Benny Hill, Charlie Chaplin and Mr Bean are known all over the world. It's when a load of water lands on someone's head or someone keeps on walking into a glass door. That's what makes people laugh. People making mistakes is always funny.
I: Do you really think so? Oh, I disagree. For me, that's not funny at all.
C: It's difficult to say. In my view, people from Argentina like a very physical humour. We like to see people in funny situations. Our TV comedy programmes have funny characters always getting into trouble and I like these. But my favourite form of humour is satire – when you get people making jokes about real things that happen, and you get comedians doing impressions of celebrities. How about you?
I: Yeah, I'd go along with that. Absolutely. In Britain there's a strong tradition of satirising politicians, for example.
D: Well, I love those old black-and-white films with Charlie Chaplin and Laurel and Hardy, and they are still incredibly popular in France.
I: Right. I see what you mean. What about other types of humour?
D: Well, because French is quite a rich language we have a lot of puns and wordplay. But I don't really like many of the jokes that I hear; I suppose it depends on how you tell the joke.
I: Yes, exactly.

Exercise 5

Absolutely!
Do you really think so?
Exactly!
For me, …
From my point of view, …
How about you?
I disagree.
I know what you mean.
I reckon …
I see what you mean.
I suppose …
I think …
I'd go along with that.
I'd have to agree with you.
I'm not sure about that.
In my view, …
Personally, …
Right.
What about …?
What do you think of …?

Exercise 7

Example:
A: I think Mr Bean is the best comedian ever.
B: I'm not sure about that.

1 A: Laughter or crying is what a human being does when there's nothing else he can do.
  B: I'd go along with that.
2 A: Comedy is medicine.
  B: I know what you mean.
3 A: What do you think of Woody Allen's films?
  B: In my view, they're very funny.
  A: Do you really think so?
4 A: From my point of view it's not the joke that's funny. It's the way you tell it. How about you?
  B: Absolutely!
5 A: I reckon comedy is a funny way of being serious. What about you?
  B: I'd have to agree with that.

Lesson 11 In the media

Exercise 3

OK. Where should I start? I'm 28 years old, and I work in media. I've always enjoyed TV, and been interested in the use of media, particularly for educational purposes. I've been working in Programme Development for about five years now, and recently I've been looking for a new challenge, a change of focus, and direction.

Well, I think in media, there is a constant need to move on to new and exciting projects. I've worked for a few different television companies now and I feel ready for the next step.

Yes, I've been working for a university TV channel called Yoonie TV. We've been trying to involve students more, by choosing programmes and topics we know they feel strongly about. Traditionally, educational programmes have been about 'talking heads', and, er, the emphasis has been much more on the academic rather than the entertainment angle. In our new programming, we've been trying to keep the balance between information content and light-hearted entertainment because students want to be informed *and* entertained.

Well, I've worked on a variety of programme types, as you can see from my CV. I've developed documentaries, and researched topics for student debate shows, um, worked on breakfast chat shows, and prepared sports interviews … Basically, I've been involved in creating shows for all genres, on different networks.

I've learnt to look at the audience, the people watching the shows. And this has helped me to develop programmes especially suited to them.

I'm dedicated and enthusiastic. I believe I can come up with good ideas, and I have the ability and organisational skills to follow them through. Also, I've always been interested in developing programmes with an educational slant, and it looks like this might be just the opportunity I've been waiting for.

Exercise 4

C = Charlie I = Interviewer

C: I've always enjoyed TV … I've been working in Programme Development for about five years now, and recently I've been looking for a new challenge …

I: What has brought about this change?

C: I've worked for a few different television companies now and I feel ready for the next step.

I: Could you tell me a bit more about your current position and exactly what you have been doing?

C: Yes, I've been working for a university TV channel called Yoonie TV.

C: Well, I've worked on a variety of programme types, as you can see from my CV. I've developed documentaries, and researched topics for student debate shows, um, worked on breakfast chat shows, and prepared sports interviews … Basically, I've been involved in creating shows for all genres, on different networks.

Exercise 7

I've been working for a university TV channel called Yoonie TV.
I've worked on a variety of programme types, as you can see from my CV.

Lesson 12 Ready to cook!

Exercise 4

1   This recipe is for Cajun Shrimp, a delicious meal from the Southern States of the USA. You will need 500g of shrimps, 50g of butter, 250ml of seafood stock for making the sauce, half a can of beer, several onions, salt, pepper and a few herbs, such as basil.

2   This dish is called chilli con carne. You will need 225g of red kidney beans soaked in cold water overnight, 750g of minced beef – that's your 'carne' which is, of course, Spanish for 'meat' – a little vegetable oil, two onions and a clove of garlic, some chilli powder, two tablespoonfuls of tomato purée, and tomatoes.

Exercise 5

To make the sauce for Cajun Shrimp, you heat about two litres of water in a pan and mix in the stock. Then chop all the onions and add them, along with a little salt and pepper, and let it simmer for at least an hour, stirring it every few minutes. For the shrimp, you need to melt almost all the butter in a large saucepan, add the shrimps, the sauce and your herbs. You cook this over a high heat for about two minutes only, stirring constantly. Then you add the rest of the butter and the beer, and you mix it for one more minute. When it's bubbling and the shrimps are tender, it should be ready to serve with rice.

Here's how to make chilli con carne. First, you put the kidney beans into a saucepan of water, boil them for ten minutes and then let them simmer for about thirty minutes. Then you heat a bit of oil in another saucepan. Not too much oil, because you don't want it to be greasy. Then add the onions and the mince. You cook these until they are brown, adding the garlic, salt, pepper and a small amount of chilli powder. Not a great deal because chilli powder is very, very hot! Then you add the tomato purée, the chopped tomatoes and the kidney beans. You should bring it to the boil and then let it simmer for thirty minutes, stirring occasionally. And then serve your chilli con carne with rice. Delicious!

Lesson 14 Two cities

Exercise 3

The city of Birmingham is located in the heart of England. Historically, it was an industrial city, but these days it has a worldwide reputation as a centre for international conferences. It is well situated and very accessible – it has one of the biggest motorway junctions in Europe, sometimes known as Spaghetti Junction, on the outskirts of the city.

With a population of just one million, Birmingham isn't a vast city, but it is a thriving one. It may not be known for its stunning beauty, but Birmingham has many attractions: firstly, it is a green city. In contrast to its image of urban sprawl, there are more parks in Birmingham than in any other European city, and it has more canals than Venice.

If you want to unwind after a hard day's negotiating, you can browse in The Bull Ring, the bustling 800-year-old market. This is renowned for its lively, cosmopolitan atmosphere and its wonderful variety of goods. Or alternatively you can stroll in the Balti Triangle, an area packed with Indian restaurants. Other highlights include the well-established City of Birmingham Symphony Orchestra and the City Art Gallery, with its outstanding collection.

If you feel the need to get away, Birmingham is surrounded by areas of beauty and interest. The countryside of Wales and Shropshire is within easy reach, and Stratford-upon-Avon, home of William Shakespeare, is less than an hour away.

With its international airport, ideal location and superb facilities, Birmingham hosts thousands of cultural and business events every year. There could be no better place for combining work and pleasure in a modern, vibrant city.

Lesson 16 Person to person

Exercise 3

Welcome to *Let's Date!* Tonight one lucky lad gets to choose from these three gorgeous girls that he's never seen before, to go on the blind date of a lifetime. We hope. You have three questions to ask …

Exercise 4

P = Presenter   D = Dean   L = Lara

P: Last week, Dean chose Lara and they went to the Red Sea for some fishing and diving in Egypt. But how did they get on? Was it love at first bite or did they just get that sinking feeling?

D: We had a great time. The diving was wonderful and so was she. Lara comes across as quite shy at first, even a little bit moody, and I wasn't sure exactly how to react to her, but once you get to know her, oh, she's got a wicked sense of humour. One time on the boat we'd been doing some fishing and I'd caught the biggest fish and I suppose I was a bit big-headed about it. Anyway, that night I went to my room and found a large, live fish in my bath. So yeah, she's the sort of person you can have a good time with. Never a dull moment.

L: The thing that strikes you about Dean is that he's so self-confident. I was a much better diver than him, but he just wouldn't believe it and he kept trying to prove that he was the best. Like when we were fishing, he kept going on about his fish being the biggest, so in the end I put one in his bath. But Dean is very cheerful and he was good company. He can be a bit opinionated, and he did keep on trying to tell our Egyptian guide about the best ways to cook fish and things like that. So there's something quite pushy about him. But basically he's very easy-going. The thing I liked about him is that he's always making you laugh and he's a bit of an idiot, but in a nice way. Yeah, I'd like to see him again.

Exercise 6

She comes across as quite shy.
The thing that strikes you about him is that he's so self-confident.
Once you get to know her, she's got a wicked sense of humour.
The thing I like about him is that he's always making you laugh.
He makes me laugh.
She's the sort of person you can have a good time with.
He's always making you laugh.
There's something quite pushy about him.
She's a bit moody.
He's a bit of an idiot.

Lesson 17 Positive thinking

Exercise 8

Example: You're sure to receive a reply soon.

1   It's possible that I'll change my job before the end of the year.
2   Average temperatures are likely to go up in the next ten years and there is certain to be a lot more rain.

3 I'm fairly convinced that life will be a lot better for my children than it was for me, as they'll have all sorts of opportunities I never had.
4 It's doubtful that computers will change our way of life much in the next few years.
5 Advances in science and medicine will certainly affect our lives. It's possible that I'll be able to live until I am over 100 years old.
6 This weekend it's bound to be sunny.

Lesson 18 Money talks

Exercise 2

B = Bruce   V = Vlad

B: I had been incredibly hard up for most of my adult life. I mean, sleeping on people's floors, doing all sorts of jobs just to pay the bills. In fact, I'd never had a proper job, so my income was always very irregular – a bit of cash here and there – but I was permanently overdrawn. Before I wrote the book, I'd never been able to afford a proper holiday or had any savings. Well, I worked hard at it for a couple of years, basically getting inspiration from my friends and from the kind of life I was living. Then, a year after I'd finished the book, I found an agent who managed to sell it to a publisher. Yeah, of course it made a difference. I have my own home now – well, I have a mortgage to pay off anyway. I'm not that well-off, but I'm comfortable and working hard on my next book.

V: The market opened up so suddenly that businesses either went boom or bust or got bought up very quickly. Previously in Russia, the easiest way to get rich was to inherit money, but now, people from all over the world were investing in Russian businesses. Foreign banks were queuing up to give you a loan. Wage demands in some sectors doubled almost overnight as people realised that 'now is the time'. Suddenly companies were giving out bonuses left, right and centre. But I don't think the ordinary people of this country, as a whole, have seen the benefits of the fall of Communism. When multinational companies make a profit, it doesn't always affect the worker, and just a few fat cats get rich. Most older Russians still live off the State pension and not much has changed for them. But it was an exciting time, and very good for businessmen like me.

Exercise 5

money well-off profit loan bonus income overdrawn

Lesson 20 Taxi!

Exercise 3

1 In Egypt, you stand by the road and you shout the name of the place you want to go to. If the driver wants to take you there, he'll stop. Then, supposing you'd shouted 'Zamalek', the driver would say 'Feyn fi Zamalek?', which means 'Where in Zamalek?' You tell him, and then he quotes you a price. And the driver will quite happily pick up other people during the journey so you can end up sharing a taxi with a family of five and a couple of chickens. It's such a great experience.

2 London's famous for black cabs and I love them. They're so comfortable, but the drivers can be fast and aggressive, so you hold on because you think they're going to crash! But they have such interesting stories about famous people they've driven, and about different parts of London, that you don't want to get out at the end of the journey! And they seem to have an opinion on every subject in the news.

3 The rickshaws you take in India are quite light, and you've got this poor, skinny man cycling away and big, fat tourists like me, with a load of luggage. I was in Calcutta a few years back, and we got stuck in the street and we couldn't move because there were all these cows in the road. And you couldn't drive them off the road because they are sacred and holy. I just remember thinking, if a car doesn't crash into us, then a cow might. It was so funny that I nearly laughed out loud. I didn't feel particularly safe in the rickshaws, but they did give you the kind of street atmosphere – the feeling that you are in the middle of this totally fascinating chaos.

4 In Thailand, taxis are called tuk-tuks. The tuk-tuk drivers come speeding up to you in the street, shouting 'tuk-tuk, tuk-tuk!' The taxis are quite low to the ground, and the top is covered, but the sides are open to let in some air, and you really need it, because it's so hot that you practically stick to the plastic seats, dripping in your own sweat. But the tuk-tuks are pretty cheap and I suppose they're quite convenient.

5 Taxi rides in Venice are so romantic. When we were there, I remember shouting 'Gondoliero!' and then a gondola arrived a minute later. We got in and they took us on this moonlit journey under bridges and between high, narrow buildings. And all the while you've got this gentle sound of the water lapping against the boat. It was such a wonderful evening!

Exercise 7

Example:
A: How was your holiday?
B: It was absolutely awful. It rained every day and I was sick.
1 A: Did you enjoy the last film you saw at the cinema?
  B: Yes. It was so good that I went to see it again the following day.
2 A: Do you like modern art?
  B: Not that much. I find a lot of it quite ugly.
3 A: Did you have a nice weekend?
  B: Yes, thanks. It was really relaxing. I lay in my hammock for two days!
4 A: How was that book you were reading the other day?
  B: It was such an interesting story that I finished it in one day!
5 A: Do you like doing housework?
  B: Not really. I find most of it rather boring.
6 A: Do you watch much television?
  B: Yes. I find the nature programmes particularly enjoyable.
7 A: Do you listen to classical music?
  B: A little, but I find most of it so boring that it usually sends me to sleep.

Lesson 21 Major events

Exercise 5

After the end of the Second World War in 1945, there was great optimism and hope that the second half of the 20th century would bring happier times. But did it? Well, the sixties was known as the 'decade of love' and man finally walked on the moon, but it also had its darker side. The Berlin Wall was built in 1961 and stayed up, a symbol of the 'Cold War' separating East and West, until 1989. In South Africa, apartheid, which had been implemented in 1948 by the South African President, Malan, grew stronger and would remain in place until 1991.

It wasn't until the eighties, however, that our eyes were really opened to great world problems. This was the decade of AIDS and of terrible drought and famine in Africa. It was also the time when we realised the environment was being destroyed, and that if we didn't stop, soon there would be nothing left. The eighties did see the birth of the personal computer, but by the end of the century, whole companies and regions were being paralysed by powerful viruses, created by individuals thousands of miles away. This has raised the fear that one day in the future, many societies will be threatened by worldwide computer viruses.

Exercise 9

Example: In 1968, black civil rights leader, Martin Luther King, was murdered.

1 In the end, the economy was rescued by the brave, handsome, Chicago-based multimillionaire, John Tomes.
2 One of the greatest technological developments, the telephone, was invented by Alexander Graham Bell in 1876.
3 It is hoped that, in the future, a cure for cancer will be found.
4 The world high-jump record, which has stood for over twenty years, was broken this afternoon by the remarkable Leslie Mbeki.
5 If pollution isn't reduced on a world scale, there will be terrible consequences for the environment.
6 The shoes, which she wore at the Milan fashion show, were made in France.
7 Sixty people have been killed in a terrible train crash in southern India.

Lesson 24 Difficult situations

Exercise 3

1 W = waiter   C = customer

W: Yes sir, can I help you?
C: Well, it's about the wine. I'm afraid it doesn't taste too good. Could you possibly bring us another one?
W: I'm sorry, sir. I'll see what I can do.

2 A = Ann   N = Neil

A: Neil. Can I have a word?
N: Yes. What's the problem?
A: I'm afraid I really need to talk to you about your attitude to work.
N: What's the problem?
A: Well, you just don't seem interested. I've had to warn you about this before, first your appearance, then being late for work, and now this. I'm afraid it just isn't good enough.

3 D = Dave   M = Marissa

D: Marissa. I wonder if I could have a word.
M: What about?
D: Well, it's about the house.
M: That again? What's the problem now?
D: Well, it's a mess. Everything's filthy!
M: What do you want me to do?
D: Well, couldn't you help tidy up a bit more? Perhaps you could do your share of the cleaning? I mean, it would be nice if you washed the dishes now and again …

4 W = woman M = man

W: Excuse me. But I'm afraid there is a queue, you know. Would you mind going to the back?
M: Oh, I'm really sorry. I didn't realise. But there are so many people in here. Why is there only one counter open? It'll take hours!

Exercise 7

Can I have a word?
I don't want to make a fuss, but you're standing on my foot.
I'm afraid I need to talk to you about your attitude to work.
It's about the wine.
It's just not acceptable.
I'm sorry, but that's just not good enough.
I really don't see why I should tidy up your mess.
I really must ask you to stop that immediately.
Would you mind going to the back?
Could you possibly bring us another one?
Couldn't you tidy up a bit more?
I wonder if you could bring me the menu?
I was wondering if you could move a little to the right?
It would be nice if you could try to keep the place cleaner.
I'm really sorry. I didn't realise.
I'll see what we can do.
I'm afraid there's nothing I can do.
I'll do my best.

Lesson 26 At home

Exercise 2

1 Warehouses like this became very popular in the nineties, in run-down areas in the heart of big cities like London and here in New York. All the young, slightly artistic-minded people like designers, and people like myself, who were fed-up with living in grotty bedsits, we bought up these run-down old warehouses quite cheaply and did them up. We turned them into these modern, live-in studios, which are very convenient for work. They're minimalist, if you like that sort of thing, and practical (they are huge so you can fit anything in them). They are airy and spacious. They do tend to be a bit draughty though, and they're difficult to keep warm in winter. I've put in wooden floors and bought a few old, second-hand rugs to make it more comfortable. Being built up high in the loft space, they have wonderful high ceilings and they let in a lot of beautiful light through the tall windows – great for artists. And they overlook the city, so the views are quite inspiring!

2 These underground houses are just north of Adelaide, in Australia. They were originally built by opal miners, who started living in the mines because it was the best way to escape from the heat. During the day, the houses stay really cool, and at night, when it's really chilly outside, inside it stays warm and cosy because of the thermal insulation. So, they're very ecologically friendly, and they're now popular with all sorts of families, because you don't need any central heating and so it's very cheap on bills. They are pretty tiny, which I think makes them romantic, but they don't have very good views. No tall windows to stare out of, so they're no good if you're claustrophobic. You can end up feeling a bit isolated.

Lesson 27 A new beginning

Exercise 4

I = Interviewer R = Romek

I: Romek, how long you have lived in the United States?
R: About five years, more or less. There are a lot of differences between Poland and the States, but I am used to most things.
I: Tell us about some of the differences. What about the people and communicating with them?
R: I'd learned British English at school and I've noticed that American English does have some differences. For example, here they say 'vacation', where in England they say 'holiday'. And the British pavement is the American sidewalk. But, generally the language hasn't been a problem.
I: What about the prices of things? Going shopping, for example?
R: In the States, things are more expensive than in Poland, but I've got used to the cost of living and I'm paid in dollars, so it's not too bad.
I: And daily life? Things like travelling around the city?
R: I used to take the tram to work in Poland, which was very cheap, but if you wanted to go out of the centre you had to drive. Here, in the States, places are more accessible because of the subway. I suppose another difference in daily life is the attitude to work. In the United States, people often put work before family. I was used to working in a more relaxed environment. Of course, people worked very hard there as well, but your free time was *your* free time, and family always came first.
I: Are there any customs here that you find strange?
R: Not really. Maybe, in Poland we normally shake hands. Here, there is a lot of kissing. But I'm getting used to it.

Lesson 28 Animal magic

Exercise 7

Examples: The kingfisher, which can't swim, dives into water to catch fish.
The penguin is the heaviest seabird which lives all year in the Antarctic.

1 The tiger, which is only found in Asia, is the largest member of the cat family.

2 Camels, which are used for trips across the desert, can drink 113 litres of water in half an hour.
3 The ostrich, which is the world's tallest bird, cannot fly.
4 Bee hummingbirds, which are the smallest bird, come from the Amazon.
5 Electric eels, which kill fish by electrocuting them, eat half their body weight in food every day.
6 The Asian elephant is the large mammal whose pregnancy lasts 22 months.
7 The anabas is the fish which can climb trees.
8 The chameleon is the lizard which can change colour.
9 The mosquito is the malaria-carrying insect which causes two million deaths a year.

Lesson 30 Growing up

Exercise 4

S = Sandra T = Tom M = Monica

S: Well, an important stage in growing up was when I chose my career, as a young adult. I decided to join the army, and I think it was a shock for everyone. I never thought I would end up as a soldier. I mean, taking on that sort of responsibility isn't always easy. And my parents weren't too happy about it either, so making my mind up about my job and what I wanted to do with my life wasn't easy.
T: I remember when my parents finally stopped telling me off the whole time, you know for everything. I suppose that must have been in my late teens. I was a reckless kid, always getting into trouble. We used to be terrible at school, always picking on the younger kids, getting them to do things for us. We were all bad, but somehow my friends always seemed to get away with it. Their parents never knew, but mine ... my mother, she would come and find me in the car. She would shout all the way home. Looking back on it, I don't know how she put up with me.
M: I remember feeling very grown up when I was about seven. My grandfather used to look after me on Sundays, and I would often sit on his knee and fill his pipe for him while he told me stories. They were wonderful stories, and I always looked forward to visiting him. Then one day, he told me I was 'too grown up for that kind of thing'. It came as a terrible shock. But I really looked up to him and believed what he said. And I remember thinking 'Well, if he thinks I'm grown up, then I really must be'.

Lesson 31 Monumental mysteries

Exercise 5

1 Stonehenge might have been some form of meeting place for tribes.
2 It must have taken about six hundred people to move each stone.
3 They could have floated the stones across the river.
4 There may've been 600 statues on Easter Island.

Lesson 32 Film reviews

Exercise 4

I = Interviewer   C = Charlotte   D = Daniel

I: Well, it opened last night, and we went along to the cinema to get reactions from those first viewers … Hello, madam, have you just seen it? What did you think?

C: Absolutely brilliant, I mean really the best film I've ever seen by a long way. The characters, the parts, were really well acted, very emotional. I love Leonardo DiCaprio. I also found it quite sad, especially that bit when the boat's sinking and she's on the deck and he's calling out to her – oh, I could hardly bear to watch. It was just so romantic. And I was dying to know what was going to happen in the end. Another thing I was really impressed by were the special effects – out of this world … they were excellent. Breathtaking. The film cost $200 million to make, but it was worth every penny!

I: Great! Thank you very much. And you, sir, could I ask you what you thought?

D: A real disappointment! Three and a half hours of romantic drivel. It was so artificial, just pathetic. The acting itself wasn't too bad, though a bit over the top at times. I couldn't stand those romantic bits on the deck. I mean the storyline was very old fashioned for a start and incredibly predictable. Terribly clichéd and a really obvious ending. They fall in love, she's rich, he's poor, the boat sinks, he's a hero – it's hardly original, is it? I suppose if you like that sort of thing, but it just wasn't for me. And the soundtrack was nothing special. I suppose the best part for me was probably the special effects, but even they weren't terribly classy, considering all the money that was spent. Definitely overrated!

I: Well, as you can see then, a mixed reaction from our viewers to this new movie …

Lesson 34 In a black mood

Exercise 5

I = Interviewer   E = Emily

I: So tell us a little about the colours, Emily. Which is your favourite?

E: Ahh. It depends on how I'm feeling. But violet is very powerful for me. It's a very strong, creative colour. Leonardo da Vinci used it to meditate, and Beethoven had violet curtains. So it's a good colour to wear when you're feeling inspired and creative.

I: And what about orange, my favourite?

E: Orange is a very energetic colour. People who are attracted to orange are people who love life. It's good if you're feeling depressed, or demotivated. If you're a bit down or feeling lonely. And just a little orange goes a long way. All you need is an orange scarf or a pair of socks, and you may feel the benefits straight away. Don't overdo it, though – it can leave you feeling restless.

I: Oh. Right. So what should you do if you're feeling restless?

E: Perhaps try some blue. It has a good calming effect on people. You can help prevent nightmares by visualising blue, and it's a good colour to wear if you're feeling frightened.

I: Yeah?

E: Or green. You wear this when you're happy with yourself, and feeling confident. It's a good colour if you're feeling adventurous and optimistic.

I: Oh. That's good to know. And red? Red must be one of the most powerful colours, is it?

E: Yes. Wear red if you're low on energy or feel cold. You can even feel warmer simply by visualising this fiery colour, but don't wear red if you're feeling agitated or nervous about something. People who like red like to be noticed. Like people who buy red cars, as a sex symbol. They actually receive more speeding tickets, because they drive fast to attract attention. They tend to be rather over-emotional, too; think about the associations of red in Latin cultures.

I: Yes, hot blooded! And what about black?

E: Ahh. Black. Women wear this to be seen as mysterious and powerful. But it can be negative, opposed to warmth and love, so it might mean you are in need of emotional support, feeling insecure. How many teenagers go through the 'black stage'? We tend to wear it when we're feeling grumpy and in a bad mood.

Exercise 7

1 inspired and creative
2 grumpy and in a bad mood
3 depressed or demotivated
4 adventurous and optimistic
5 a bit down or feeling lonely
6 naturally tranquil temperament
7 feeling restless
8 tend to be rather over-emotional
9 insecure and in need of support
10 agitated and nervous

Lesson 35 Missing the mark

Exercise 4

I = Interviewer   J = John

I: John, tell us about a few more predictions that have gone wrong.

J: Well, one particularly rich area is predictions about inventions and technical developments. For example, in 1943, Thomas J. Watson, chairman of the board of IBM, announced that there was a world market for about five computers. And in 1977, Ken Olson, the president of Digital Equipment Corporation, calmly assured the World Future Society that there was no reason for any individual to have a computer in their home. Even Bill Gates, in 1981, claimed that 640K would be enough for anybody on one computer.

I: Amazing.

J: And that's just computers. Before that, we had all these other fantastic inventions, and people – even intelligent people – just couldn't see them coming. Charlie Chaplin promised us that cinema was just a passing fashion. And just as the first films with sound were arriving, Harry Warner of Warner Brothers refused to see their potential. 'Who the hell wants to hear actors talk?' he said.

I: And these were people right at the cutting edge of their industry.

J: Exactly. The co-founder of Rolls Royce warned the world that he didn't think flights across the Atlantic were possible. And H.G.

Wells, the great science-fiction writer, confessed that he couldn't see submarines doing anything but suffocating their crew at sea, due to the lack of air. All these predictions were proved wrong just years or even months after they were made. But I think the king of the wrong prediction was a man named Lord Kelvin. Lord Kelvin was a mathematician and physicist in the 19th century. He predicted that the radio had no future. He also argued that flying machines which were heavier than air were scientifically impossible. And X-rays were his third great mistake. He denied that they were possible, too.

I: And what about other areas, besides inventions?

J: Yes, I think in every area of man's existence people are constantly putting their foot in it, saying quite ridiculous things. Politicians are particularly good at this.

I: Aah.

J: It was Margaret Thatcher, of course, who pointed out in 1969 that no woman in her time would be Prime Minister. But even she couldn't match a certain Mr Reagan when it came to ludicrous statements and predictions. At the height of the Cold War, Ronald Reagan insisted that there wasn't even a word for 'freedom' in the Russian language. He also tried to persuade the American public that a year's waste from a nuclear power plant could be stored under a desk.

I: Figures in public office …

J: Figures in public office. You'd think they would be a bit more careful.

Lesson 37 The dream business

Exercise 2

I = Interviewer   M = Martin

I: Martin Johnson, you're in charge of the jazz section of www.musicmaker.com, the online music store that lets customers put together their own selections on CD. Can you tell us a little bit about your responsibilities within the company?

M: Yes. Musicmaker's jazz section consists of hundreds of jazz tracks, and I'm responsible for helping customers find a particular track and also encouraging them to invest their time – and money – in artists that are maybe new to them. So I'm a sort of online guide to our jazz collection.

I: And what's your main task?

M: Well, I take care of the organisation of the music, so that everything is in the right place: big-band tracks next to other big-band tracks, smooth jazz tracks with other smooth jazz tracks. I specialise in jazz at our site, but my expertise extends to hip-hop, R&B and pop music. Obviously, as Jazz Editor at Musicmaker, that's what I have to concentrate on. I'd also say that I often highlight the work of great but lesser-known artists like Lee Morgan and Booker Ervin because I am concerned about such musicians, whose work might be overlooked because they aren't currently in fashion.

I: Can you tell us about the actual contact with customers? Is it all via e-mail?

M: Yes. Every day I handle dozens and dozens of e-mails. I think it's important to deal with customer questions as quickly as possible. But, of course, a lot of the e-mails are from my fellow editors or my boss. I liaise with them on a day-to-day basis. And yes, I really do depend on my computer and Internet service provider.

I: Are there any annoyances or problems with the job? It sounds perfect for a music lover.

M: I have to cope with silly enquiries from our customers, some of which seem designed to get on my nerves. But that's just part of the job. And perhaps surprisingly for a dot-com company, we also use a lot of forms, which I have to sort out and file. But yes, it's a great occupation. When I resigned from my previous job to begin working at Musicmaker, it might have seemed like a big risk, because Musicmaker was new and challenging. But all of us here are proud of what we have achieved.

Lesson 39 I wish …

Exercise 4

1   I was in an Italian restaurant in London once, when I noticed that, sitting behind me, was Pelé, you know the Brazilian footballer. He'd been my childhood hero, so I was very excited. I really wanted to say something to him, to get to know him, but I was too shy. I couldn't think of what I wanted to say, and before I knew it he'd paid his bill and left the restaurant.

2   I'd been playing with this group, The Bugblatters, for years. We worked hard and we really wanted to make it big, become famous. But it just wasn't happening. I got impatient and disillusioned and I decided to give it up and get an office job. I needed the money. The funny thing is, six months after I left, they got a contract – they made their first CD and then toured all over Europe. And I'm still working in the same boring old office.

3   I had a boyfriend when I was younger who asked me to marry him. We were both very young at the time. We'd been childhood sweethearts. We went for this long walk one day, up to the castle in Edinburgh, and when we got to the top, he proposed. I don't know why but I just panicked. I still had so much to see, so I turned him down. Oh, it was a big mistake. He soon left me and found another girl, but I never stopped loving him.

4   I worked for an antiques dealer for a couple of years, and I was second to the boss. He was fairly old, and he always talked about retiring. He wanted to give up work and move to Italy. As Assistant Manager, naturally I'd have been promoted to run the company. Anyway, he kept putting it off and putting it off and I was always there waiting. Eventually I decided to leave and start my own company. It wasn't an easy decision to make, but I couldn't wait forever. And then about a year later, he did retire, and of course someone else got the promotion.

Exercise 6

1   I was in an Italian restaurant in London once, when I noticed that, sitting behind me, was Pelé, you know the Brazilian footballer. He'd been my childhood hero, so I was very excited. I really wanted to say something to him, to get to know him, but I was too shy. I

couldn't think of what I wanted to say, and before I knew it he'd paid his bill and left the restaurant.
If only I hadn't been so shy. I should have asked him for his autograph.

2   I'd been playing with this group, The Bugblatters, for years. We worked hard and we really wanted to make it big, become famous. But it just wasn't happening. I got impatient and disillusioned and I decided to give it up and get an office job. I needed the money. The funny thing is, six months after I left, they got a contract – they made their first CD and then toured all over Europe. And I'm still working in the same boring old office.
I wish I'd stayed with the band. I shouldn't have taken this job.

3   I had a boyfriend when I was younger who asked me to marry him. We were both very young at the time. We'd been childhood sweethearts. We went for this long walk one day, up to the castle in Edinburgh, and when we got to the top, he proposed. I don't know why but I just panicked. I still had so much to see, so I turned him down. Oh, it was a big mistake. He soon left me and found another girl, but I never stopped loving him.
If only I hadn't panicked. I shouldn't have turned him down.

4   I worked for an antiques dealer for a couple of years, and I was second to the boss. He was fairly old, and he always talked about retiring. He wanted to give up work and move to Italy. As Assistant Manager, naturally I'd have been promoted to run the company. Anyway, he kept putting it off and putting it off and I was always there waiting. Eventually I decided to leave and start my own company. It wasn't an easy decision to make, but I couldn't wait forever. And then about a year later, he did retire, and of course someone else got the promotion.
I wish he'd retired earlier. I should've waited another year.

Exercise 9

Example:
A: I don't believe it!
B: What's wrong?
A: We've been burgled! If only I hadn't left the window open.

1   A: Oh, no! I've burnt the pie!
    B: How did you manage that?
    A: I fell asleep.
    B: Hmm. Perhaps you shouldn't've gone to watch TV.

2   A: I was there at the top of this mountain, with my camera.
    B: Fantastic.
    A: But then I realised I'd run out of film.
    B: Oh, how annoying! I bet you wish you'd checked before you left.

3   A: How was the holiday?
    B: A disaster. We lost all our luggage, and we don't have any insurance. I wish we'd taken out insurance now.

4   A: So he split up with Sarah, who was lovely, and married Elaine, who was awful. And then they got divorced after two terrible years.
    B: Poor man! If only he'd stayed with Sarah in the first place.

5   A: All my flowers have died. I can't understand it.
    B: Did you water them?
    A: Yes, every two months.
    B: Maybe you should've watered them a little more often.

6   A: Have you decided which flights to get yet?
    B: Yes, and I've bought the tickets, but they were more expensive than last week.
    A: Oh, I knew we should've booked them earlier.

Lesson 40 Mind your manners

Exercise 2

1   A: Good evening.
    B: Hi.
    A: Is anyone sitting here?
    B: No.
    A: Would you mind if I joined you?
    B: Not at all. That would be lovely.
    A: Can I get you a drink?
    B: That's very kind. I'd love one.

2   A: It was lovely to see you again, Sue. We really enjoyed ourselves. Thank you so much for having us to stay.
    B: Not at all. It's a pleasure.
    A: But it was really kind of you to put up with all of us and the animals.
    B: It's no problem at all. You must come again soon.
    A: Thanks for the offer. We'll do that. See you again soon then!
    B: Yes. Have a good trip.

3   A: I passed!
    B: Oh, well done … at last! Congratulations! We'll have to celebrate.
    A: Yes. How about opening a bottle of champagne?
    B: Brilliant idea.

4   A: Do you fancy coming with us to the theatre to see *Murder in the Garden*?
    B: I would, but you'll never guess what. My sister saw it yesterday.
    A: Really?
    B: Yes, and I'm afraid she said it wasn't very good.

5   A: Oh, I'm sorry, madam.
    B: Oh, don't worry about it.
    A: That was really very stupid of me. Let me apologise.
    B: That's fine. It's perfectly all right.
    A: But your shirt!
    B: It's no problem. I'll …

Exercise 4
As for Exercise 2, but with pauses for students' responses.

Practice section answer key

1 Getting ahead

1 1 took up 2 been into 3 sacrifice
4 do for a living 5 achieved her goal
6 were lucky enough to

2 1 I **went** to Brazil last summer. It was
wonderful.
2 This evening, I **am going** out to dinner in a
small, local restaurant.
3 I always **enjoy** eating good food.
4 In my life, I **have been** travelling many
times.
5 I **meet** people every day through my work.
6 I **started** studying English when I was at
school.
7 I **met** him when I lived in Asia.
8 This weekend I **am going** to see an art
exhibition.

3 1 started; was 2 had; inspired
3 have; loved; was 4 Have; had
5 won; am showing 6 Have; enjoyed
7 was living; became
8 Do; have (*Have*; *got* also acceptable)
9 am working 10 am going to open
(*would like to open* also acceptable)

2 Modern survival

1 1 exhausting 2 relaxing 3 clean
4 stressful 5 polluted 6 unhealthy

2 1 cut down 2 working out
3 in good shape 4 gave; up
5 balanced/healthy 6 relieving stress
7 put; weight

3 1 stressful 2 polluted 3 work out
4 exhausting 5 relaxing 6 cut down on
7 balanced diet 8 gave up

3 Coincidences

1 1 simultaneously 2 later 3 Whenever
4 previously 5 eventually 6 lately
7 often 8 as soon as

2 1 had been living 2 wanted 3 decided
4 had told 5 had been travelling
6 (had) expected 7 had been staying
8 got 9 was having 10 saw 11 jumped
12 had calmed down 13 was crawling
14 hit 15 had never been 16 got back
17 discovered 18 had gone 19 had found
20 had stung

4 Friends

1 1 classmates 2 workmates 3 flatmate
4 penfriend 5 boyfriend
6 fair-weather friend

2 1 although 2 as a result 3 despite; too
4 However 5 On the other hand

3 Suggested answers
1 We could buy an expensive new sofa; on
the other hand, we could just keep the old
one.
2 My car is very old; because of this,
sometimes it doesn't start first time.
3 My suitcase is very heavy, therefore I
would rather use the lift.
4 Businesses are not only cutting costs, they
are also increasing prices.
5 I ordered a new computer over a month
ago; as a result, I expect to receive it by
the end of the week.
6 I told him I didn't want to book the room;
he is sending us a brochure nevertheless /
nevertheless, he is sending us a brochure.

5 Small talk

1a 1 chat 2 small talk 3 interrupting
4 in deep conversation 5 invite
6 moaning 7 criticised 8 say goodbye

1b a 2 b 8 c 5 d 6 e 7 f 3 g 4 h 1

2 1 d 2 j 3 a 4 i 5 g 6 b 7 c 8 h 9 e
10 f

6 True love

1 1 They got together at university.
2 They had a happy marriage.
3 It lasted a long time.
4 They had a lot in common.
5 They got divorced.
6 They were in the public eye.
7 They spent time apart.

2 1 ✔
2 ✘ We first came **across him** at a party.
3 ✔
4 ✘ Good. I'm glad you didn't **split up (with
her)**.
5 ✘ She has been ill for ages but I think
she'll get **over it**.
6 ✘ I get on well **with** my parents.

3 1 splitting up 2 made up 3 make-up
4 was getting on 5 taken; to
6 come across 7 got on 8 fell out
9 get over 10 got back

7 The daddy of discipline

1a 1 b 2 c 3 f 4 h 5 d 6 g 7 a 8 e

1b 1 They are playing truant/taking time off
school.
2 They are doing chores/odd jobs in the
house.
3 They are getting into trouble/being
naughty.
4 They have got caught/have got into trouble.

2 1 need to 2 shouldn't 3 had to
4 mustn't 5 oughtn't to 6 must
7 should

8 That's funny

1 1 The Beatles were the top band of all time,
I agree.
2 *Revolver* was their greatest album. **I'd go
along with that**.
3 **The thing** (that) I like about Bob Dylan is
his early albums.
4 I know **what** you mean.
5 I love David Bowie's songs. **How about
you?**
6 **In** my view, Bob Marley should be on the
list.
7 What do you think **about** Pink Floyd?
8 I think that Nirvana's album isn't as good
as Pink Floyd's.
9 I **don't** agree with the top five albums.
10 **According to** *The Times*, The Beatles are
better than Oasis.

2 1 Personally, I see no other solution.
2 I'm not sure about that.
3 I'd go along with that.
4 Do you really think so?
5 From my point of view, that's true. / That's
true from my point of view.
6 I see what you mean.
7 I'd have to disagree with you.
8 I agree, but in my view it helps.
9 Absolutely! But what do you think of his
latest film?

9 A perfect weekend

1 Across: 2/6 people watching 9 the Net
10 stay in 11 housework

Down: 1 window 3 exercise 4 lie-in
5 clubbing 7 catch up 8 DIY 10 surf

2 1 are coming to 2 are going to 3 arrives
4 will collect 5 aren't coming
6 are planning 7 is 8 will have

10 Just the job

1 1 communication 2 experienced
3 motivate 4 organisational
5 co-ordinating 6 managerial
7 ran; research
8 a good eye for detail

2 Suggested answer

> **Betta Pharmaceuticals plc**
>
> ### Chief Executive Officer
>
> As a result of a complete restructuring of the organisation, we are now looking for a new CEO to take the company forward. The successful candidate will be an innovative and highly experienced manager. He/She will have excellent communication skills and the proven ability to motivate departments and co-ordinate the process of restructuring change.
>
> The position involves running the existing business whilst researching and developing a strategic plan for further expansion.

11 In the media

1

```
M Y K I N O S T C G H P Z
U N I Q U I Z S H O W E R
S A D O H N E A A N I R U
I N O T U M O R T E T U B
C O C O M E D Y S H O W D
O U R S E R Q H V M I E
H I M P S O A P O P E R A
A X E L P A M S W I M E D
N O N E O F A N Y S J D V
N A T U R E S I C W B G E
E L A L T T H R I L L E R
L A R I S R Y C O Y S H T
S O Y D H C A R T O O N S
```

1 music channels 2 chat show
3 documentary 4 drama 5 adverts
6 quiz show 7 comedy show
8 soap opera 9 nature 10 cartoons
11 sports 12 thriller

2 1 been running 2 won
3 been watching; finished 4 been cooking
5 caught 6 found

12 Ready to cook!

1 1 melts 2 Pour 3 Chop 4 Add
5 serve 6 Fry 7 simmer 8 roast 9 boil
10 Stir

2 1 not much 2 a bit of 3 Every few
4 Most 5 a small amount of 6 much
7 some 8 a large number of

3 1 There's *not much* beer left over from the party.
2 *Not many* of us are hoping to go to university after school.
3 On the news, it said there *was a great deal of* trouble on the streets.
4 Did you eat *a little* cake at the party?
5 *A large number of* the programmes on TV are worth watching.
6 *A large amount of* money was found under the bed when he died.
7 Too *few* people are worried about the environment.

13 Contact

1 1 shake hands 2 cross your fingers
3 hold hands 4 kiss; cheek
5 shrug; shoulders

2 1 to leave 2 going 3 having 4 shouting
5 to let 6 to open 7 to visit
8 to understand

3 1 pretended 2 expected 3 chose
4 attempted 5 managed

14 Two cities

1 1 renowned; accessible 2 thriving
3 the outskirts 4 reputation
5 cosmopolitan 6 vast 7 well established
8 stunning

2 1 vibrant 2 Located 3 easily accessible
4 stunning 5 renowned 6 in the heart of
7 vast 8 well-established 9 bustling

15 Round the clock

1 1 burn the candle at both ends 2 early bird
3 work round the clock
4 burn the midnight oil 5 works long hours
6 am a night owl 7 a split shift

2 1 have; will go 2 won't get; sees
3 cook; will do 4 will let; promise
5 would call; knew 6 were; would ask
7 have; find 8 call back; will; ask

3 1 When I **go** to Lisbon, I will definitely send you a postcard.
2 John gets paid more if he **works** overtime.
3 The world **would** be a better place if something was done to reduce poverty.
4 If he **calls** me late at night, I am usually still awake.
5 If I **pass** my exam, I will be so happy.
6 I would get really bored if I **lived** in the country.
7 If it **was/were** my house, I **would** paint it all different colours.
8 If they **get** back in time, we can still watch the match on TV.
9 As soon as she **sees** the sun, she gets a tan.

16 Person to person

1 self-confident, easy-going, dull, opinionated, cheerful, big-headed, sensitive, moody, thoughtful, pushy

```
H I S T I R C L O W B N I K S L
A S E L F C O N F I D E N T U R
V T N O G M U G G L I X J H F U
E A S Y G O I N G R A T U O U O
T W I S B O L L I N G A D U L L
H A T P P D U S N A R C O G L H
E T I Q U Y S A G G A K W H Y P
R C V E S O P I N I O N A T E D
C H E E R F U L K I R S T F S O
H Z X R E A S S B D B N O U T T
O M M B I G H E A D E D A L E X
P U D D N S Y W A K T O D P M V
```

2 1 pushy 2 dull 3 self-confident
4 big-headed 5 easy-going 6 sensitive

3 1 Julian comes **across** as very shy, but once you **get** to know him, you realise he's quite self-confident.
2 She starts crying as soon as you criticise her! She's **a bit/very** sensitive.
3 The **thing** I like about Helen is that she is always cheerful.
4 She's the **sort** of person who can be very opinionated.
5 He always thinks about other people's feelings. There's **something** very thoughtful about him.
6 He puts a lot of pressure on his workers. He is a bit **of a** pushy boss.
7 The first thing that strikes **you about** her is that she is very moody.
8 He is very **big**-headed. He is always going on about how great he is.

17 Positive thinking

1 1 hot-tempered 2 bright and breezy
3 dull 4 chilled out 5 warm

2 1 There's a fair chance that you
2 you are bound to
3 would imagine (that) you
4 You definitely won't
5 You are convinced (that)
6 It is possible (that) you will
7 You are sure to 8 You will probably
9 are certain to
10 It is doubtful (that) you will
11 It is likely that you

18 Money talks

1 Across: 1 pay off 5 loan 6 invest
7 inherit 9 overdrawn 12 afford

Down: 1 profit 2 income 3 pension
4 well-off 8 hard up 10 earn 11 wage

2 1 afford 2 paying off the mortgage
3 paying the bills 4 well-off 5 profit
6 invest 7 bonuses 8 pensions

19 Unlucky for some

1 Suggested answers
1 The car has been written off.
2 The car has broken down.
3 The waiter has tripped up.
4 She is filling up the car with petrol.
5 She is cheering him up.

2 1 was going to drive 2 was about to
3 was due to 4 was on the point of
5 about to 6 was due 7 was about to

20 Taxi!

1 1 so 2 little bit 3 such 4 slightly 5 so
6 such 7 quite 8 totally

2 1 so 2 really 3 pretty 4 so 5 such a
6 rather 7 fairly 8 absolutely 9 so

21 Major events

1 1 d 2 f 3 b 4 e 5 c 6 a 7 g

2 1 made 2 was crowned 3 sank
4 was assassinated 5 seized 6 attended
7 was founded 8 was caused 9 was led
10 began 11 declared

3 1 was assassinated 2 has been discovered
3 will agree 4 beat 5 will be awarded
6 are built 7 has been found

22 Street life

1 1 c homeless person 2 d street vendor
3 b pedestrian 4 e busker
5 a fortune teller

2 1 take their time 2 hadn't taken
advantage of 3 hasn't taken place
4 won't take any notice / will take no notice
5 take you by surprise 6 I took for granted
7 get to know 8 get crowded 9 to get to
10 had always managed to get around / had
always got around

23 Gun crazy

1 1 shoplifters 2 pickpockets 3 burglars
4 Muggers 5 smugglers 6 kidnappers

2 1 had told; would have helped
2 had arrived; have been able
3 had been; would have crashed
4 wouldn't have got; hadn't been
5 would have gone; hadn't been
6 wouldn't have come; had known
7 wouldn't have married; had told
8 wouldn't have realised; had come; hadn't
knocked

24 Difficult situations

1 1 My food/cheese is mouldy. It needs
throwing away.
2 My shirt is torn. It needs mending.
3 My bedroom is messy. It needs tidying.
4 My TV doesn't work. It needs repairing.

2 1 Do you think you could possibly open the
window, please?
2 I'm sorry, but that's just not good enough.
3 I'm afraid I need to talk to you about your
appearance.
4 I'm afraid there's nothing I can do.
5 It would be nice if you could remember it
this year.
6 I don't want to make a fuss, but you
haven't done the dishes for six weeks.
7 I'll see what we can do.
8 I was wondering if you could lend me a bit
of money.
9 I really must ask you to put out that
cigarette.
10 Would you mind turning down the music,
please? / Would you mind turning the
music down, please?

25 Under pressure

1 1 It annoys me when I forget what I was
about to say.
2 It drives me crazy when I can't find my
keys.
3 It irritates me when people aren't polite.
4 I find it stressful when I have to meet
deadlines at work.
5 It's a relief when you don't have to go to
work on Sunday.
6 It's comforting to know that he'll ring me
when I arrive.
7 People who are big-headed really get on my
nerves.

2 1 are slowly coming to realise
2 are becoming more interested
3 are more and more common
4 is increasingly aware
5 is still going
6 is starting to come down
7 not following the trend
8 is becoming more and more difficult
9 is catching on
10 are more often driving

26 At home

1 1 central heating 2 overlooks 3 convenient
4 modern 5 huge 6 brand-new
7 minimalist 8 wooden

2 1 warm 2 wooden 3 huge 4 minimalist
5 garden 6 ceiling

3 1 tiny 2 huge 3 spacious 4 loft
5 basement 6 classic 7 high ceilings
8 wooden 9 modern 10 chilly
11 fireplace 12 cosy

27 A new beginning

1 1 gas station 2 freeway 3 apartment
4 garbage 5 subway 6 sidewalk
7 stand in line 8 movie

```
S T A N D I N L I N E
M Y P H U B S K B I I
S G A S S T A T I O N
F A R H I E M O G S T
R R T M D P O R A T A
E B M T E S U B W A Y
E A E E W R S O A N I
W G N M A Y L I Y F E
A E T N L D I A D O R
Y H I M K O M O V I E
```

2 1 d 2 f 3 a 4 b 5 e 6 c

3 1 get used to 2 didn't use to
3 get used to 4 am; used to 5 are used to
6 used to 7 get used to 8 is; used to

28 Animal magic

1 1 whose 2 which/that 3 why 4 who
5 which

2 1 Ghost stories, which exist in most countries
and cultures, have been told for hundreds of
years. / Ghost stories, which have been told
for hundreds of years, exist in most
countries and cultures.
2 The poltergeist is a type of ghost which/that
does naughty things like throwing objects
around a room.
3 Borley Church is the famous haunted church
in England where ghosts have been seen
and strange noises have been heard.
4 The writer Martin Green was walking in
Wales in 1979 when he saw the ghost of a
World War II plane in the sky.
5 A young couple, Carla and Thierry, and their
son, Jean, who lived in Mulhouse, France,
had a poltergeist in their home for three
years.

3 1 The girl who ~~she~~ gave me the money
disappeared.
2 ✔
3 ✔
4 The day **which/that** I like best is Saturday.
5 The film, which was made in Hollywood**,**
was very popular.
6 John Grisham is a writer **whose** books have
made him millions of dollars.
7 Shopping**,** which is my favourite hobby**,** is
more fun in big cities.
8 ✔
9 I saw a photo of the church **where** / **in
which** my parents got married.

29 Treat yourself

1 1 I drink coffee to keep me going.
2 A good movie always cheers me up.
3 Swimming calms me down when I'm
feeling stressed. / When I'm feeling
stressed, swimming calms me down.
4 Flowers usually make me feel better

2 1 having/getting (OR going to have/get) our
bathroom painted tomorrow.
2 had my temperature taken when I was in
hospital.
3 having/getting my computer repaired.
4 got her car insured before she went on
holiday.
5 have/get our newspapers delivered every
morning.

3 Diane has had the lamp repaired.
the floor cleaned.
the curtains replaced.
the sofa moved.
the chair removed.
her nails painted.
her hair cut.

30 Growing up

1 1 f 2 g 3 c 4 e 5 b 6 h 7 d 8 a

2 1 end up 2 get away with 3 tell us off
4 picking on us 5 looked up to
6 looked forward to 7 made up
8 looking after

31 Monumental mysteries

1 1 weighs 2 high 3 depth 4 height
5 length 6 Deep

2 1 can't have 2 must have 3 could have
4 might have

3 1 it might have been 2 can't have been
3 must have been 4 he could have been

32 Film reviews

1 Across: 3 suspense 7 overrated 8 script
10 breathtaking 11 location

Down: 1 world 2 supporting
3/4 special effects 5 star 6 soundtrack
8 setting 9 like

2 1 a bit over the top
2 I can hardly bear to watch
3 it was worth every penny
4 They were absolutely out of this world!
5 if you like that sort of thing

33 Making life easier

1 1 breaking 2 causes 3 reliable 4 wasting
5 save 6 help; run

2 1 have sent 2 be relaxing 3 be working
4 have been sold 5 be waiting
6 have escaped

3 1 will have been created 2 will be using
3 will have become 4 will be living
5 will have happened 6 will be working

34 In a black mood

1 1 tight-fitting 2 striped 3 trainers 4 plain
5 suit 6 baggy 7 patterned 8 high heels

2 1 nervous 2 grumpy 3 restless
4 over-emotional 5 tranquil 6 optimistic
7 inspired 8 lonely 9 demotivated

35 Missing the mark

1 1 a) assure b) deny c) announce
2 a) insist b) predict c) point out
3 a) claim b) warn c) confess

2 1 warned him not to go
2 announced (that) she was
3 assured Julie (that) he would
4 denied eating / denied (that) he had eaten
5 pointed out that
6 claimed to have / claimed (that) he had
7 promised to / promised (that) she would
8 predicted (that) they would have

36 Now or never

1 1 cook book 2 manual 3 guidebook
4 encyclopaedia 5 biography 6 diary
7 autobiography 8 thriller
9 volume of poetry

2 1 Not knowing where to go, I asked a
stranger on the street.
2 Running is the best thing you can do to
keep fit.
3 Opening the door, I realised why she loved
that room.
4 Having lived here for two years, we know all
the local people.
5 I like the actor playing the part of Vladimir.
6 The interviewer asked many confusing
questions.
7 Knowing John, I can tell you he would
prefer to watch ballet.
8 He saw the girl standing by the lake.
9 Swimming in the sea can be so dangerous.

3 1 c Seeing the open window, the burglar
climbed into the house.
2 e Standing close to the fire, the boy was in
danger of getting burnt. / The boy
standing close to the fire was in danger
of getting burnt.
3 f Not coming from this country, I don't
know the customs very well.
4 b Having failed to find her phone number, I
will have to visit her at home.
5 a The wind blowing in the west soon
became a tornado.
6 d Running in the park one day, I bumped
into an old friend.

37 The dream business

1 1 in; of 2 in 3 with 4 for 5 of 6 with
7 out 8 on 9 about

2 1 resigned from 2 had invested in
3 It depends on 4 to concentrate on
5 I've taken care of 6 consists of
7 am not proud of 8 liaise with lots
9 be concerned about
10 has been in charge of

38 Fingers crossed

1 1 He's being nosy.
2 He's giving him the elbow.
3 He's trying to catch her eye.
4 He's got his hands full.
5 She's giving him a hand.

2 1 will keep my fingers crossed
2 don't see eye to eye
3 make up your mind / make your mind up
4 (have) had my hands full
5 will catch his eye
6 have been (getting) out of hand
7 broke my heart 8 is getting on my nerves
9 on the other hand 10 Learning by heart

39 I wish ...

1 1 turned down 2 put off 3 come off
4 missed out on 5 let me down 6 set out
7 sign up for

2 1 a) I wish I had known about the bus.
b) I should have taken the bus.
2 a) I wish I had bought a ticket last month.
b) I should have booked a ticket.
3 a) If only I had checked the food.
b) I shouldn't have eaten that chicken.
4 a) If only I had spoken when I had the
chance.
b) I wish I had been able to practise more.
5 a) I wish I had said no when I was first
offered a cigarette.
b) I shouldn't have started smoking.
6 a) If only I hadn't sold it.
b) I should have kept my flute.

40 Mind your manners

1 1 A: Do you fancy going to the theatre
tonight?
B: Thank you for the offer, but I'm busy
tonight.
2 A: You'll never guess what.
B: What's happened?
A: I've been offered that job.
B: Congratulations!
3 A: It was really kind of you to look after my
pet.
B: It was a pleasure.
4 A: I'm sorry, but I've lost those shoes you
lent me.
B: It's no problem at all.
5 A: It was lovely to meet you.
B: See you again soon.

2 1 f 2 a 3 e 4 g 5 b 6 c 7 i 8 j 9 d
10 k 11 h

3 1 3e 2 7i

Pearson Education Limited
Edinburgh Gate, Harlow
Essex CM20 2JE, England
and Associated Companies throughout the world.

www.language-to-go.com

Language to go is a trademark of Pearson Education Limited.

First published 2002
Third impression 2006
Set in 9/12pt Neue Helvetica Medium and 9/12pt Univers Light
Printed in China. SWTC/03
ISBN-10: 0-582-40399-5
ISBN-13: 978-0-582-40399-4

Author acknowledgements

The authors would like to thank all the students and teachers at the London School of English and International House, London for their inspiration and encouragement, and also Bernie Hayden, Catriona Watson-Brown, Judith King, Simon Greenall, Frances Woodward and Suzanna Harsányi for all their input, patience and expertise. Special thanks also to Charlie Clare, Chris Wilson and Andrea Sabbatini.

Publishing acknowledgements

The publishers would like to extend thanks to the freelance editorial team. We are indebted to Bernie Hayden, Senior Development Editor for the whole series, for his outstanding contribution to *Language to go*. Special thanks are due to Catriona Watson-Brown for her exceptional work, particularly as project manager and editor on this Upper Intermediate level, and on all the Phrasebooks in the series. We would also like to acknowledge with thanks Kenna Bourke for her writing of the Grammar reference.

The publishers and authors are very grateful to the following people and institutions for reporting on the manuscript:

Christopher Reakirt, The New School of English, Cambridge; Nanna Challis, Frances King School of English, London; John Murphy, Swan Stratford, UK; Philip Dale, Hampstead School of English, UK; Rolf Donald, Eastbourne School of English; Henny Burke, The British Language Centre, Madrid; Robert Armitage, IH, Barcelona; Sarah Bailey, Lexis Instituto del Idioma, Málaga; James Tierney, The British Council, Milan; Mark Trussell, IH, Milan; Anne Vernon James, IFG Langues, Paris; Philippa Dralet, Le Comptoir des Langues, Paris; Jennie Kober, Anglo English School, Hamburg; Shaun Wilden, Akcent, IH Prague; Tim Banks, Akcent, IH Prague; Jodi Bennett, The Language House, Prague, Czech Republic; Andrew Edwins, Warsaw; Adam Kunysz, The Catholic University of Lublin/A1 School of Foreign Languages, Poland; Cleide Silva, São Paulo, Brazil.

We are grateful to the following for permission to reproduce copyright material:
the University of Alabama at Birmingham for an extract adapted from 'A brief overview of Birmingham', published on www.uab.edu; Steven Appleby for the cartoon 'Suddenly, I awoke one morning to find I'd become a grown-up', published in *Guardian Weekend*, 24th April 1999; Atlantic Syndication Partners for an extract from 'Why Britain suffers a kissing crisis', published in *Metro* 12th May 1999, and adapted extracts from 'John Hind on coincidence', published in *ES Magazine* 28th May 1999 and 'John Hind on bad weeks', published in *ES Magazine* 20th August 1999; Cover Magazine for a fictional interview based on the article 'Missing the mark' by Dermot Purgavie, published in *Cover* Issue 21st June 1999; the author, Maureen Freely, for an adapted extract from her article 'The daddy of discipline', published in *The Observer* 21st February 1999; Independent Newspapers (UK) Ltd for adapted extracts from 'Working around the clock' by Lynne Butt, published in *The Independent* 18th February 1999 and 'Work should always be a complete joke' by Cherry Norton, published in *The Independent* 16th August 1999, and The Week for an adapted extract from 'Gun Crazy', published on www.theweek.co.uk.

Layout by Newton Harris Design Partnership

Series design by Steve Pitcher

Cover design by Juice Creative

Author photographs on the back cover by Trevor Clifford (bottom) and James Walker (top)

Illustrated by: Rowan Barnes-Murphy (12–13, 82–3), Gary Bates (36–7), Paul Collicutt (26, 27), David Downton (70–1), Noel Ford (9, 15, 23, 25, 29, 31, 35, 41, 43, 45, 49, 55, 57, 59, 65, 67, 73, 75, 77, 79, 81, 83), Jon Hamilton (76–7), Paul Hampson (8–9, 28–9), Matthew Herring (72–3), Peter Lubach (68–9, 87, 89, 91, 94, 96, 97, 99, 100, 102, 103, 104, 106, 107), Louise Morgan (55), Flatliner (48), Peter Richardson (74, 75), Debbie Ryder (5, 15, 38, 68), Geoff Waterhouse (40, 41, 50, 51, 78–9), Gary Wing (47).

Picture research by Sally Smith

We are grateful to the following for permission to reproduce copyright photographs:
Art Directors and Trip for 33 top, 63 top, 80 right and left, 81 top and bottom; Bubbles for 60; Camera Press for 18 top and 32–33; Cephas for 4 bottom middle and 39 top left; Bruce Coleman Collection for page 33 bottom; Corbis Stock Market for 6 top; Corbis UK Ltd for 4 top middle; Empics for 23 left; Eye Ubiquitous for 35 background and 54 bottom; Format Photographers for 10 right, 32 bottom and 62; Ronald Grant Archive for 5, 19 right, left and middle; Sally and Richard Greenhill for 7 top and 17; Robert Harding Picture Library for 64 bottom left and top right; The Hutchison Library for 42 top left and bottom left; Image Bank for 56 right and left; Image State for 20 bottom, 30 bottom, 42 right, 43 top and bottom, 46 main, 47 inset, 54 top, 58 right, 59 and 65; Kobal Collection for 67 bottom; Magnum for page 32 top; Moviestore Collection for 25 top right, 66 left and right; Network Photographers for 33 middle; Pearson Education/Trevor Clifford for 34 and 35 overlay; Pearson Television for 25 bottom; The Photographers Library for 57 and 61 top; Pictor International for 7 bottom, 30 top, 46 inset and 47 main; Popperfoto for 20–21 and 52; Powerstock Zefa for 20 top, 23 right, 24 left, 38 left and right, 39 bottom right and 63 bottom; Press Association for 4 top left, 23 middle and 45 top; Retna for 4 bottom right, 11, 45 bottom and 67 top; Science Photo Library for 44 top and bottom and 58 left; Still Pictures for 6 bottom; Telegraph Colour Library for 4 bottom left, 24 right, 25 top left, 61 bottom right; Thoughtful Books for 16 bottom left; Topham Picturepoint for 14 right and left and 18 bottom; John Walmsley for 4 top right, 10 left, 16 top right and top left; The Week for 49.

Front cover photographs left to right: Image Bank; Corbis Stock Market; Image State; Corbis Stock Market; Telegraph Colour Library